SHOULDERS FOR OUR CHILDREN
A Spiral Becoming

Shoulders For Our Children
A Spiral Becoming

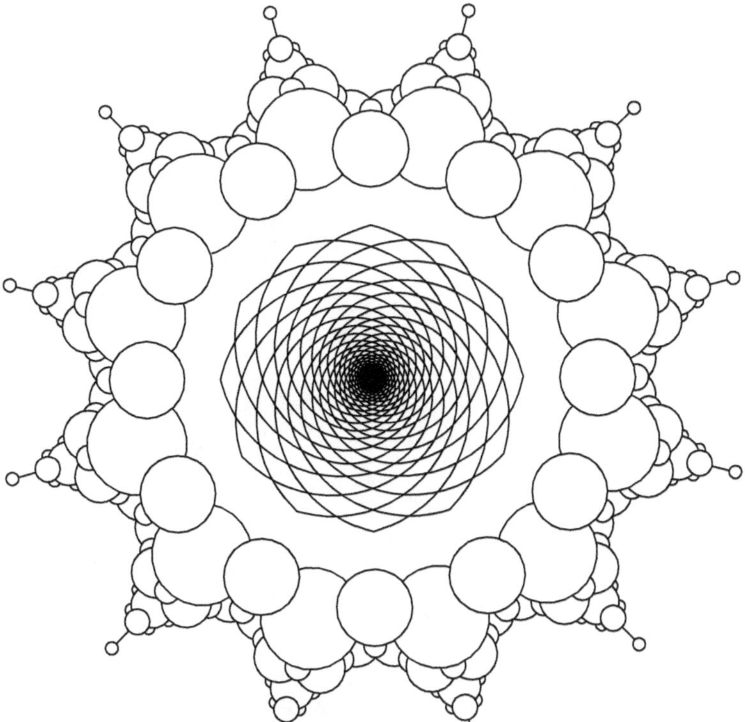

Shoulders for Our Children can be read in its entirety at:
www.SofianBooks.com

Copyright © 2016 Sofian Books LLC

Shoulders for Our Children by A Spiral Becoming is licensed under a Creative Commons Attribution-NonCommercial-ShareAlike 4.0 International License. To view a copy of this license, visit http://creativecommons.org/licenses/by-nc-sa/4.0/ -- or contact Creative Commons at 171 Second St, Suite 300; San Francisco, CA 94105 USA (phone +1-415-369-8480).

Catalogue-in-Publication Data
Shoulders for Our Children/ A Spiral Becoming 1. Civilization 2. Culture 3. Mysticism 4. Metaphysics 5. Spirituality 6. Reality, model of.

ISBN-13: 978-0997473209
ISBN-10: 0997473207

May these shoulders that once carried you be useful to you again, giving you an elevated perspective so that you may see further and with more clarity, rising above the distractions that will so often surround you. Climb upon these aging shoulders one last time. Stand upon them and see what we who proceeded you could not.

What follows are these shoulders in words – words that are not intended to stamp upon your mind a set of beliefs, but words that are meant to stir your own becoming so that you might notice, if only for a moment, the existence of a more expansive reality that stands before you. Let these shoulders be no more than a foundation upon which you can build. If you find cracks or find that the foundation is not deep enough, fix it, go deeper and rebuild.

Contents

Lesson 1.	Crude Approximations	1
Lesson 2.	Sacred Proportions	3
Lesson 3.	The Story of Moloch	5
Lesson 5.	Sphere of Agriculture	11
Lesson 8.	Sphere of Money	15
Lesson 13.	Law of Technique	22
Lesson 21.	Sphere of Acquisition	31
Lesson 34.	Sphere of Governance	37
Lesson 55.	Sphere of Distraction	45
Lesson 89.	Sphere of Indoctrination	53
Lesson 144.	Building Blocks of Language	61
Lesson 233.	Sphere of Certainty	69
Lesson 377.	Moloch in Their Eyes	85
Lesson 610.	Overcoming the Beast	99
Lesson 987.	Story of the Spirals	103
Lesson 1597.	The Sacred Point	109
Lesson 2584.	Learning Environments	117
Lesson 4181.	Necessary Evil	121
Lesson 6765.	Cycle of Necessity	125
Lesson 10946.	Purpose	133
Lesson 17711.	Experience	139
Lesson 28657.	Humility	143
Lesson 46368.	Truth	147
Lesson 75025.	Spirals in Your Eyes	153
Lesson 121393.	The Path of Attention	165

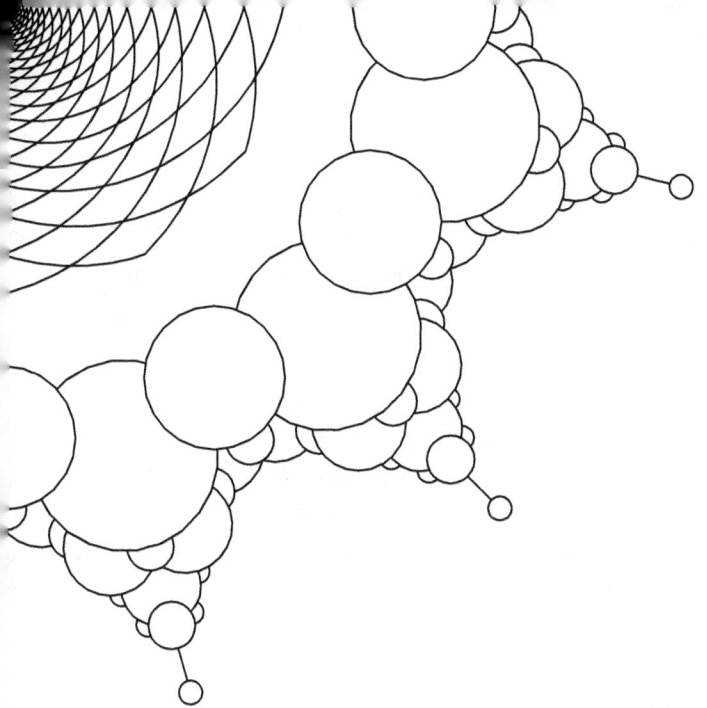

Lesson 1

Crude Approximations

Imagine a blank canvas from which penetrates a single point. It is a true point, having no dimensions, by its very nature unmeasurable – nothing and everything, zero and infinity. Within this abstraction lies pure and infinite potential. However, the actualization of this potential requires movement, the stepping down through division of one point into the many points of possibility.

Movement results in the emergence of innumerable spirals. The composition of these spirals is mysteriously a collection of these dimensionless points that have arranged themselves into stable patterns of beautiful relationships. The existence of these spirals creates upon this canvas both an outward and an inward movement in relation to the point that gave birth to them.

As these spirals move further away from their source, they eventually must go unseen, concealed by a necessary emptiness that gives way to a great multitude of ever evolving and expanding spheres. These spheres are all different, and yet, they are all the same. They are all connected, and yet, they are all separated.

This image will be your guide to everything that follows. It is a map that will help you see the danger in maps. For what follows, whether found in word, number or image, are mere abstractions – crude approximations of a reality they so desperately try to point to.

Symbols are necessary models of reality we create to aid us in communication and understanding, but as with all maps, they are not what they point to. Therefore, whatever it is, it isn't, and whatever a map may claim to be, it is not. The trouble lies in merely holding on to symbols as opposed to what those symbols point to, forgetting that we are the creators of these maps. This image and the words that follow are simply pointers, and what they point to is what you must learn to uncover.

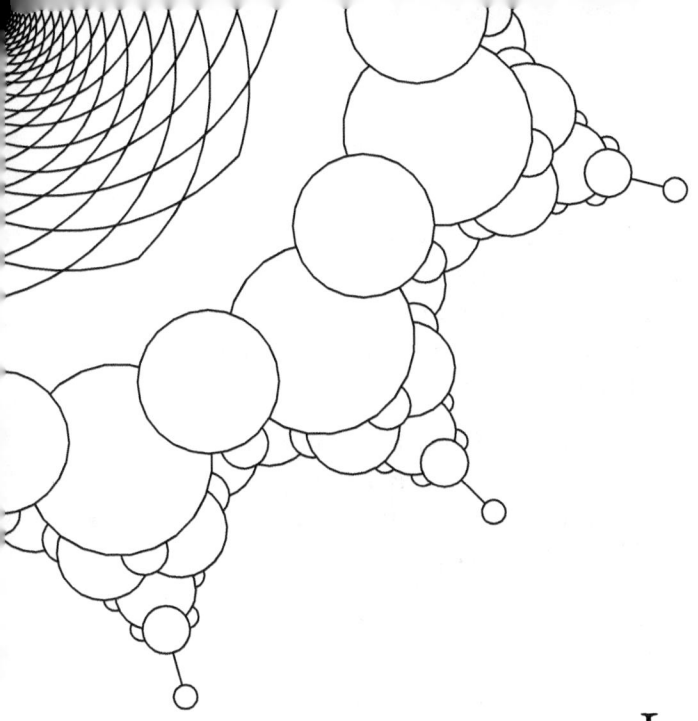

Lesson 2

Sacred Proportions

Our complex realm of existence is presented to us as an amazing whole, and from within this whole we find ourselves to be an individuated part. When examining parts and how they relate to the whole, we are dealing with proportion. Proportion is defined by the relationship between parts and their corresponding wholes.

There exists within this realm an archetypal pattern of motion that compels us to learn from the balanced relationships that it creates and maintains. This proportion has been called the golden ratio, and it is this ratio that not only unites its many parts so as to preserve their own unique identity, but it also perfectly aligns these individuated parts in order to create and preserve the identity of the whole. When this relationship between parts and the whole is maintained, we have the very definition of harmony and balance, which is intuitively admired for its beauty.

To spend time with this beautiful relationship of motion, is to discover a marvelous lesson hidden within. When encountered, this lesson will present the listener with two questions: How do we, as a part, relate to the whole, and how does the whole relate to its many parts? Do these relationships possess harmony and balance in their proportions, the intuitive beauty of a golden spiral, or do they embody disproportion, imbalance and instability, possessing neither beauty nor harmony?

To gain understanding we must begin with the first question: How do we, as a part, relate to the whole? How we relate to the whole is largely determined by the ongoing stories that we carry within. Stories are the images and ideas that direct our thinking and give shape to our perception of the world. They are the unconscious producers of action that are so deeply woven within the fabric of our minds that they are rarely even noticed. Our unconscious stories must be made conscious, for only then can we experience the mystery of how the whole relates to its many parts.

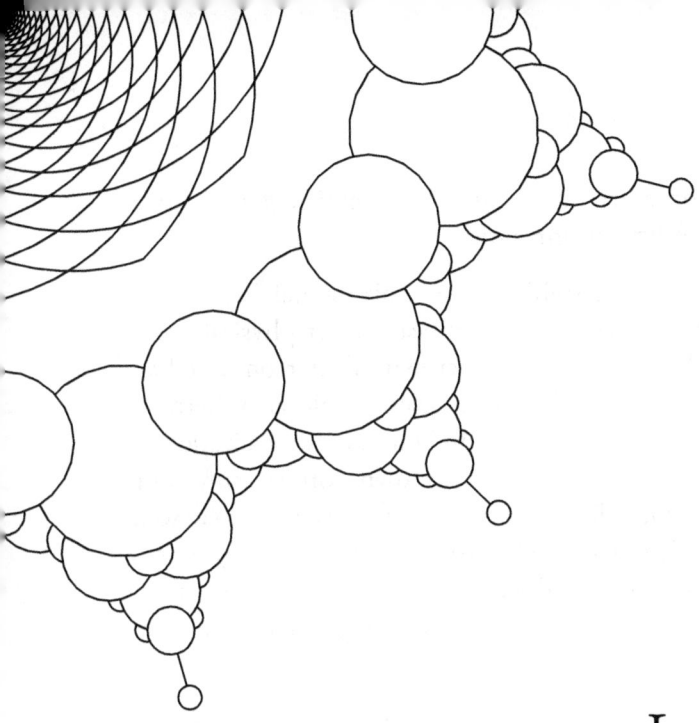

Lesson 3

The Story of Moloch

There exists a city that is not located on any map. It has no physical location, as it only resides within the properties of the mind. But do not think that this city is unreal, for it is as real as any physical city, possessing the power to not only create reality for those whose minds it resides in, but also for those in whose minds it does not. This city has been given many glorious names by its residents; but to those who have defected, it has, with much caution, been given the name of Moloch – the place of great sacrifice. It is here, within this mental city, that humanity has sacrificed what it most essential, for everything that is unessential, giving up an expanding reality for unrealities.

If it were possible to view this mental city from an elevated perspective, it would appear to our physical eyes as something like a metastasizing crown of interconnected and overlapping spheres of varying sizes. While all spheres are similar in their appearance, all differ in their specializations, as each sphere tends to express its own sort of autonomy, functioning much like its own district. If we were to descend into one of these spherical districts and peer through its fog-like haze, we would discover that the structure of this metastasizing crown is really a sprawling mass of towering structures.

Regardless of the particular district, Moloch's towering structures are all architecturally congruent, each having been built upon massive pillars that rise out of a great expanse of water. This is no ordinary water, for it is troubled water that has been agitated and cloaked in darkness in order to keep the inhabitants of these districts from traveling upon it. Though rarely is this water even inquired about due to the astonishing display of multicolored lights that purposely illumine the interconnected structures above. These lights exist to mesmerize the masses. They are enchanters that seek to forever maintain the gaze of Moloch's residents.

It would be impossible to make an itemized account of Moloch due to its enormous size and evolutionary nature, and here-in lies its seductive power, as it is able to evade total scrutiny, forbidding comprehensive inquiries and allowing only superficial and fragmentary surveys. Nevertheless, in spite of its complexity, we do know that within each of the structures there exists a multitude of floors that hide within them a multitude of reality tunnels. These cave-like environments have been set up in such a way that if, by chance, a resident finds their way out of one, they will almost certainly find themselves unknowingly within another. Due to Moloch's transformative nature these deceptions know no limits. New structures are constantly created and existing structures are constantly remodeled, generating an almost impenetrable illusion of free movement.

These cave-like environments are the mental structures that occupy our minds, surrounding us with shared images that shape our perceptions of what is real. It is here, in these caves, where we find the birthplace of our forgetting, as it is here where we have slowly grown accustomed to shared stories and limiting perspectives, unquestioningly accepting our homogeneous environment and our place within it. And it is here, in these caves, where we most often find ourselves, comfortably seated, forever staring at an artificially illuminated wall with all those who have gone before us.

Caves and their supporting structures exist for all of us. They are many different things to many different people, and yet, they each tend to function in very similar ways. At their most basic level, caves discourage us from questioning the fundamental premises by which we live, allowing us to be content, blindly accepting distortions that are presented to us as reality. Their very structure serves as perfect environments for the creation and perpetuation of unconscious automatons whose only opinions are the ones supplied to them and whose only thoughts are the unending reflections of acceptable groupthink. Within these cave-like environments there are no quiet places to develop an intuitive story from within, as everything is a deafening surface of polished veneers that condition residents to ignore, dismiss and sometimes destroy any attempt at new information that might damage their shared illusions.

The structured environments of Moloch are, by design, growth inhibitors that leave us vulnerable to those who delight in taking advantage of the led. To live in this city is to become a commodity of this city, being ownable, exploitable, controllable and useful insofar as we are able to maintain conformity. Similar to well-trained animals, we are kept passive and obedient through rewards and punishments, salivating over our need for more, striving for greater power, status and control, grading ourselves by a hierarchy of our own making and daily convincing ourselves that the distorted really is the norm. As a result of cave living we ultimately become disconnected to any new reality beyond our cave, being content with the artificial, with the mundane and with things that have no vital interest to us for the span of our short life.

Inevitably, caves teach us to fear the darkness and uncertainty that lies beyond. To go bumping around in the dark, we are told, means things will bump back, inflicting untold damage to ourselves. And so we submit and conform, unquestioningly accepting the comfortable seats that the cave provides. These seats are acceptable forms of existing that keep us thinking and acting in ways that maintain the separated self in a socially constructed artificial realness. It is here, in these seats, where we interact with a mass of like-minded people, creating beliefs and making decisions based solely upon what can be learned within our own restricted environments, within our own limiting perspectives, unable to comprehend that something much larger may lie beyond our respective caves.

Preventing us from recognizing these environments is our propensity for distractions, artificial illuminations that serve to enhance the cave's appeal, fixating our eyes on everything that is pleasurably unessential. These artificial illuminations are human inventions of inconsequential trivialities that control our life, providing the mind with enough unrealities to avoid the thing that would inevitably result if these distractions were removed; the question of why?

It is this very question that can begin to take down the mirrors our cave environments give us, and it is this question that holds within it the potential to cause us to turn from the wall and its reflections and to notice, if only for a moment, the existence of some new reality behind us. When glimpsed, it will forever gnaw at the self, until at last, we can do no more than release our controlling grip and quietly venture out into the terrifying darkness that has beckoned us. It is here, within this humbling darkness, where we inevitably begin to discover a host of great teachers who have been patiently waiting for us all along. These teachers find us in the darkness and bump back, painfully teaching us of their existence.

The teachers we find in the darkness are the many spirals that emanate from the point. Although Moloch must shroud them in darkness, their beautiful lines extend even into the darkest cave, drawing us in by their unseen mechanisms, teaching us of the existence of another type of structure that quietly sits beneath the city. This structure is called a boat, and its makeup is completely different than the towering structures of Moloch. It is not fixed, it moves when you least expect it, and it carries you to places you cannot foresee or control. It is, by its very nature, unpredictable, as it possesses no rudder and follows no well-defined path; yet somehow, in its own time, it takes you to where you need to be.

There are some who will find this boat tethered to a particular structure, only to discover the troubled water it sits upon. Out of fear, they will immediately find themselves scrambling back to the nearest structure of safety, control and predictability, unable to comprehend a reality beyond the jurisdiction of Moloch.

But for you, do not let go of this boat, for even though it will, at times, seem like the most unstable of structures, if you persevere, it will eventually carry you to unimaginable places. The journey into greater realization cannot proceed until peace is first made with uncertainty, mystery, and doubt.

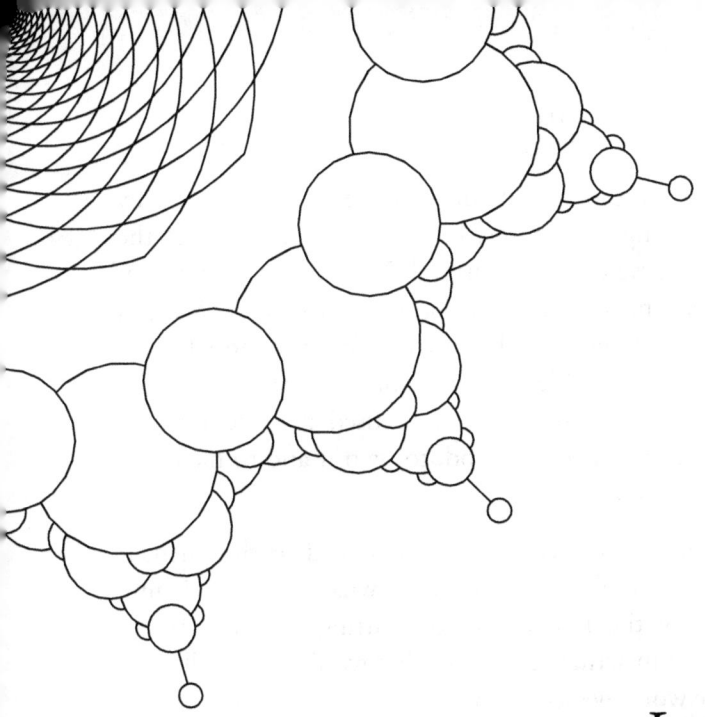

Lesson 5

Sphere of Agriculture

The mind in which the city of Moloch dwells is a separated mind. It is a part that has forgotten its relationship with the whole. Separation creates Moloch thinking – a perpetual cycle of self-centered actions that project the mental spheres and structures of Moloch into physical reality. Through the conduit of Moloch thinking, this mental city and its constructs are able to cross the barrier of the mind. For when Moloch is in the mind, it can do no more than actualize its story of control into physical reality.

One of the first mental spheres to be created by Moloch thinking was centered on food, as it is one of the most essential elements to survival. Within the ideology of Moloch, food must be controlled by the strong. As Moloch thinking began to grow within, man eventually chose to pass over the uncontrollable free gifts of food that the earth provided for him. Instead, man focused his attention on finding ways to control his food, to own it and to make the earth work for him.

Believing himself to be an overlord of the earth, it only seemed natural to take control of what belonged to him. Therefore, by the first action of putting the land under cultivation, man actualized a force that would eventually give birth to the world we see today.

Infected with even the smallest traces of Moloch thinking, it was inevitable that humans would seek to manipulate those parts of nature that were viewed as separate from themselves. In their minds the world became an 'other,' seen only in the light of its usefulness to man.

With this new thinking of separation implanted within, humans did what no other species had ever done before: they denied the community of life access to food. This was done by clearing and destroying whole ecosystems in order to make room for only their food. Any species within this new quarantined area that interfered with the production of human food, were quickly destroyed. This was the first step of domestication, bringing the free and uncontrolled plant realm under control for self-serving purposes.

As the human connection to nature continued to weaken, animals also started to be subjected to an imposed hierarchy of interspecies relationships. With man as their overlord, animals came to be seen as separated objects – unfeeling machines to make meat and milk. Yet nature, ever the great teacher, did not condone the lordship of man over these realms.

When man planted crops, weeds and insects would destroy them. When he stored food, mold and rodents would spoil them. When he held animals captive, other animals like the hawk, fox, and wolf would liberate them. When he constructed, the rain and the wind deconstructed. When he gave himself a diet of meat and milk, disease gave him an early grave.

Man did not learn from the error of his thinking. Instead, he scorned his teacher's lessons and worked harder, stored smarter, bred and built even stronger. Instead of relating to nature as a beautiful teacher, man sought to force upon nature his own will. Instead of cooperating with nature as a friend, man sought to compete against it as an enemy.

As the war progressed and man attained success in taming certain grasses and animals, storable and tradable commodities began to appear. Land, seed and animals all came to be seen as the product of hard work, something to be stored, corralled and exchanged. With domestication came excess. Excess meant wealth, and wealth meant control. These instinctively served to focus man's attention on what enacting the story of Moloch would give him but blinded man to what the story of Moloch would eventually take away from him.

Whereas before, man had a very intimate relationship with the flora and fauna; however, as this new story played itself out, man began to lose the necessary relationships that had earlier enabled him to live free.

In believing that the world around him was insignificant, man set himself on a course to also be made insignificant. He was unable to see a system of his own creation slowly developing around him that would eventually have the power to also deny him free access to food. Ultimately, what man did to others, he did to himself.

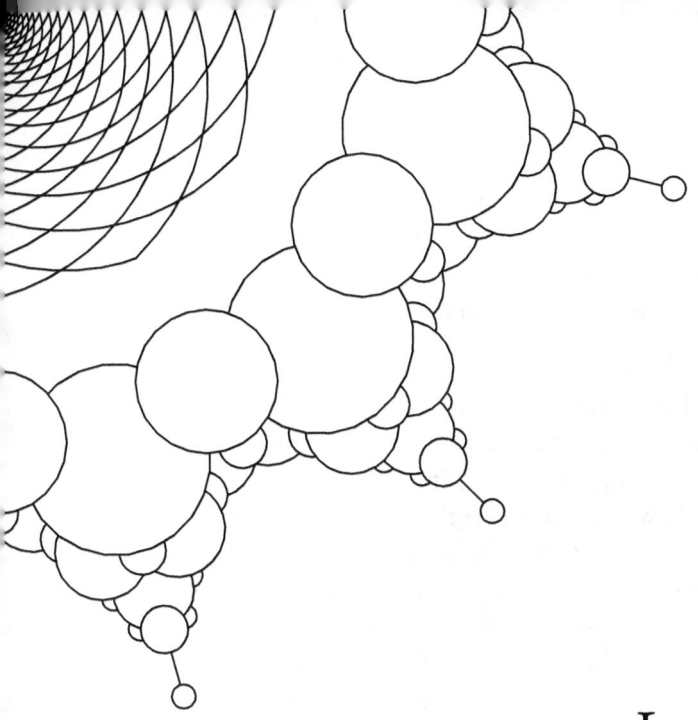

Lesson 8

Sphere of Money

All material wealth is essentially theft. Man did not make the plains, hills, valleys, mountains or rivers. In claiming ownership over them, he essentially created a new concept called theft. The first theft happened when man simply decided to take, separating various parts from the community of life and placing them into the realm of 'mine.'

Regardless of its forms, ownership points to the deep malady of separation that lies within. It is a malady that perceives the world as a thing to be owned, controlled and manipulated. Ownership is nothing more than a projection of this unconscious story of Moloch that we enslave ourselves to, a mere agreement between humans that allows us to become takers and claim ownership over this earth.

As the spheres of Moloch grew around the minds of men they began to see the world only as a collection of objects to be owned, and thus, another concept called money, was created. Money is a belief. It is something that becomes real the more we believe it is real. Money has value because it is attached to a story that gives it value. Regardless of the form it takes, whether it is a piece of gold or a piece of paper, money remains a product of this unconscious story, another projection of Moloch thinking that gives us permission to believe these objects and ideas are worth pursuing.

Money is an illusion, as are all the projections of Moloch thinking. But, this illusion is one of the most powerful kinds. It exists outside and above the rules of nature. It does not decay and it does not return to the soil like everything else. Money exists perpetually as a growing and invisible force. In order for money to be a force, it needs people to believe in it. When a sufficient number of people are convinced of its worth, money then becomes power and control – the very objects of worship for the residents of Moloch.

The result of living within this particular mental sphere is inevitably a life that requires constant competition for its very survival. This can be most clearly seen in the debt based systems that have been designed to use the power of ownership to take more from others. The trap with any debt based monetary system is that all new money, by design, comes from interest bearing debt. This system creates the need for perpetual growth, as new money must be made in order to pay off the interest bearing debt. Competition is permanently built into these systems.

To see this more clearly, look at how a modern human buys a house. First, they go to those who control the belief, borrowing 100,000 units of money that will have to be paid back over 30 years along with the interest that the 100,000 units has incurred. Due to the added interest, at the end of 30 years, the buyer of this house will have paid back around 300,000 units of money to the controllers. The question becomes: Where did this extra 200,000 units come from? To service this debt, new money had to be created. New money is almost always created by taking it from the community of life. This taking is simply the conversion of the natural, cultural, social and spiritual world into goods and services that, through various processes, can then be turned into money. Debt, by design, will always be greater than the supply of money. This insufficiency of money causes its users to be in constant competition with everybody and everything. To be wealthy in the realm of Moloch requires that the community of life must be made poor.

As these monetary systems of belief have evolved and grown, they have had to become exceedingly complex in their functioning. For this reason, humans have given this illusion over to economic storytellers, a priesthood of financiers. This priesthood does what all priesthoods do: the work of manipulating minds. Followers of this priesthood are encouraged to sacrifice more and more time to the God of money for the promise of a future heaven. The priests increase their money and power by virtue of having money, simply because they create it and you do not. The laity increase their faith in money, believing that it is sacred and will fix all their problems. Naturally they come to worship it and will devote their life to the production of it.

Belief in this illusion compels us to participate in a way of thinking that must increasingly convert all aspects of this world into money. This mental sphere requires continuous and limitless growth for its very survival – it must either grow or die. Since death is not an option for Moloch thinking, it must grow at the expense of everything else. Money can facilitate this growth because it is an abstraction, a symbol in the form of numbers that has no limit. Money, like numbers, has seemingly infinite growth potential.

Inevitably, what results from enacting such a system of infinite potential is an uncontrollable fire that must spread in order to survive. In order to spread, it must consume more and more fuel, which is the expanding of more goods and services, finding more and more things to turn into money. This fire consumes everything that is beautiful, and when it has finished, all that will be left is money.

Moloch thinking, by separating various parts from the community of life and placing them into the realm of 'mine,' gave birth to the material illusion of money. This material illusion has grown to become such a powerful force that man now uproots the world in a desperate attempt to be somebody, sacrificing his precious span of life to the pursuit of more. Man can no longer see the marvelous around him, because in its place he has created a world that mirrors his mental city, a machine of steel, smoke and slavery, hidden by a thin veneer of lights and polished surfaces that compels him to live in a distracted and mechanical state.

Within this unbalanced environment, parts that are an essential piece of this great spiraling whole are viewed as being separate and disconnected – 'others' that are only seen for their usefulness in making money and markets. As a result, man's relationship to the community of life has devolved into a world that blinds him from noticing the incredible spirals that quietly exist beneath this matrix of illusion.

If we could quiet our minds, we would hear the voice of Moloch as it whispers through its halls, "just a little bit more and things will be better." This voice is the echo of ideology, a potent drug that offers up money as the cure to a disease that money created. To pursue this drug is to ensure that it will retreat faster than we can approach it, enslaving ourselves to the continual pursuit of more.

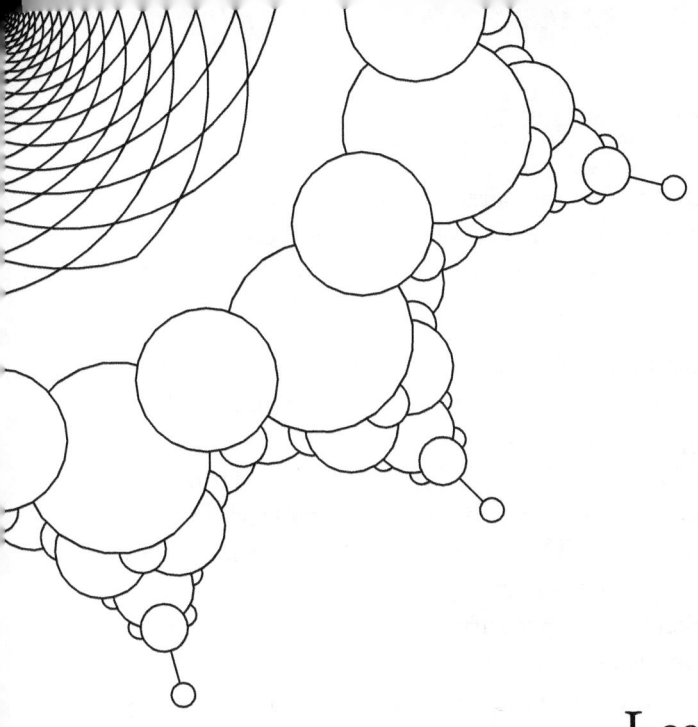

Lesson 13

Law of Technique

It is here that we must step back for a moment and examine an essential law that ensures the orderly and rapid expansion of this mental city and its innumerable spheres. To exist within the realm of Moloch is to be bound by a law which mandates that all of our efforts must be directed to the most efficient means of fulfilling our self-centered desire for more. This unseen law is a blind force that structures and patterns the way we think, committing ourselves to continually improved means that aim at carelessly examined ends. To submit to this law, is to find ourselves always moving, always chasing after the most efficient ways to acquire more: more control, profits, resources, objects, safety, security, distractions and certainty. This law is called Technique.

One unique characteristic of the law of Technique is that it always strives for autonomy. Even something as simple as a digging stick, when placed under the law of Technique, follows the mandate to evolve into a hoe and mattock, for these refinements improve efficiency, clearing more land and planting more seeds. These tools had no choice but to evolve into the plough, first driven by animals, then by steam and then by diesel and electricity, as these, too, were simply further improvements of efficiency. Eventually, these tools arrived at a point where they could do no more than compel the destruction of previously unthinkable amounts of land. How could a resident justify not overturning large swaths of land with such a capable and expensive tool? Tools that were once under the control of their users, through increased efficiency, ended up drawing the user under the control of the tool – all for the promise of more.

With both eyes on what Technique would give him, man had no eye on what it would take away from him. This Faustian bargain served to focus man's attention on what it would do while simultaneously obscuring what it would undo. Technique gives, but never in equal measure, to what it takes away. By accepting this bargain, man naturally fixated on the short term successes that Technique gave him. Perfecting the digging stick really did increase yields. Tilling the soil did release more nutrients. Planting a single crop over large areas did make it easier to manage. Confining animals to small spaces did make it more efficient to get meat and milk.

And cutting down trees did produce more money than leaving them alone.

With each short term success, the idea was reinforced that humans, indeed, had the power to control and master the world through following this law. Therefore, man, without hesitation, put supreme faith in the idea of progress, believing that these small steps would eventually lead to a technical utopia where technical means would cure all his ills. Whatever consequences man found along the way, and whatever sacrifices Technique required of him, were easily justified by this illusion of heaven that these short term achievements promised him. He believed in Technique's promises to such a degree that he completely immersed himself within this matrix, directing all his efforts towards the pursuit of technical improvements. With each improvement, man could not be satisfied, for with Technique it is never enough.

Let us take as an example the human desire for food. With Technique, the questions become, how do we make the production of food more efficient and how do we compel humans to eat more of it? The answer under Moloch thinking will always be: more control through increased efficiency. We will grow monocultural foods, tilling up and planting large areas with a single crop. When nature tries to warn us of our folly by giving us lifeless soil and sending insects, weeds and disease to destroy our crops, we will not listen; rather, we will develop new management solutions. We will use the soil as an inert medium to hold the roots so that nutrients can be poured on top. We will create insecticides, herbicides and fungicides, even to the point of altering the plant's genes so that they can tolerate much stronger chemicals. Then, we will take this food and process it in a factory, combining it with cheap fillers like sugar, salt, fat and a host of chemically derived ingredients to keep people from realizing that they are full.

Again, nature tries to warn us of our folly by sending a host of lessons like lethargy, autoimmune deficiencies, sickness and depression. But, do we learn? No. Instead, we allow the chemicals that laden our food to be renamed into something that we do not recognize. We accept the cheaper and more efficient genetically modified foods, and most importantly, we work for these things and put them into our mouths. This cycle creates new health, water and agricultural giants who profit from the declining health of everyone and everything; yet, we accept more and more of these technical applications because to do otherwise, would mean a loss in our own profits.

Another example is the human desire for meat and milk. Technique mandates that the production of meat and milk must increase at all costs and this is accomplished through more control and increased efficiency. We will tear down trees and grow out large grass lands to feed the animals. When there is not enough grass or land to sustain the livestock, we will develop more efficient practices. We will coral them into smaller areas, and even cage them so that they cannot move. We will then feed them massive amounts of cheap corn to quickly fatten them up. When nature tries to warn us of our folly by giving us diseased, oppressed, and exploited animals, we will not listen; rather, we will develop even more efficient management solutions. We will medicate the animals with antibiotics, we will feed them vitamins and minerals that they do not receive from corn, and we will fill them with growth hormones so that their animal flesh and their milk will come to market even quicker. Then we will take this flesh and milk and process it with chemicals to sterilize it for the masses.

Again, nature tries to warn us of our folly by sending a host of lessons like obesity, heart disease, diabetes, cancer, sickness and depression. But, do we learn from these lessons? No. Instead we blame our violent ends on our poor gene expression, poor exercise habits, and poor luck all the while increasing our consumption of these violent delights. This cycle creates more and more industries that profit from the declining health of all involved. But it is never enough, and so we accept more and more of these management solutions and technical applications because that is how it has always been done.

Technique can be found in the human desire for sweeteners. Honey becomes a commodity that is made by honey bees, and so the question becomes, how do we make more honey? The answer under Moloch thinking will always be: more control through increased efficiency. We will breed bigger and better bees by putting them into our own vertical hives. We will give the bees artificial comb with extra-large cell spacing. We will feed them sugar to replace the honey that we take from them. We will remove the male drones for their perceived uselessness.

Oh but nature, ever the great teacher, tries to warn us of our folly by sending a host of lessens our way. Mites, pests, fungi, bacterium and viral diseases come to plague our hives. Bees are dying and colonies are collapsing. But, do we learn? No. We implement more control, dousing our hives with acids, pesticides and fungicides. These controls continue to produce unforeseeable consequences that will require even further management. This cycle creates new industries and agrochemical companies who profit on the declining health of the bees and the beekeepers, who must now use more and more technical applications to keep their hives alive and their money flowing. We create the problems that we think we are fixing. As the problems grow, so do the solutions. This creates more problems and more solutions; however, as the story goes, with just a little bit more control we will one day arrive at the perfect production of more honey.

The same process works itself out with our human desire for fruit. Fruit becomes a commodity that can be grown. The question becomes: how do we make fruit bigger, more appealing and unblemished? The answer under Moloch thinking will always be: more control through increased efficiency. We will breed better trees, graft onto better root stock, propagate seedless strains, prune, fertilize, thin blossoms, and create monoculture orchards.

Oh but nature, ever the great teacher, tries to warn us of our folly by sending a host of lessons our way. The caterpillars, sawflies, aphids and weevils converge. The moths and birds come to feast. Scab, canker and rot, move in to weaken and destroy the fruit and tree alike. But, do we learn? No. We implement more control. We spray with chemical fungicides and bactericides. We clear around the base of the tree for sanitation. We remove spoiled fruit from the ground. This cycle creates new industries and agrochemical companies who profit on the declining health of the trees and organisms that eat the fruit. Now, the producer of fruit is forced to use more and more technical applications or lose all of their fruit trees and their money. We create the problems that we think we are fixing. As the problems grow, so do the solutions. This creates more problems and more solutions; however, as the illusion goes, with just a little bit more control we will one day arrive at the perfect production of more fruit.

At present, man has become hooked on the technical fix, unable to contemplate reversing his course. To do so would mean his yields and his profits would plummet. It is never enough. With his mind infected by Moloch thinking, he has become complicit in his own destruction, having to poison his food and his environment just so he can eat. Faith in Technique has only served to cloud man's perception. Instead of stepping back, man seeks to progress and is forced to seek out more actions to fix the problems that his previous actions have already created. The tool no longer becomes a means that is serving an end; rather, it becomes the end that must now be served because of how it has altered the natural, social and psychological environments in which it has arisen.

This directing force is not limited to the agricultural sphere, but is found in every sphere and in every structure. Each technical action brings on new advances and adds new technical difficulties, which demand more advances. Unforeseeable problems will always develop as a result of any new action, and with no way of figuring out all of the potential repercussions, man will only have time to react with some new technical fix, remaining trapped in this deceptive loop.

Our addiction to Technique is really no different than an addict's addiction to a drug, for destruction finds its door through the diminishing returns of increased use. In the same way that an addict must use larger and larger doses of a drug just to feel normal, so too does our society pursue more and more doses of Technique in order to keep this system functioning. It must be understood that, with any addiction, it is the drug that is creating the symptoms that the addict thinks it's treating.

Technique cannot be fixed and it cannot be reformed as it is deeply embedded within the mindset of Moloch. Any attempt to do so will simply create another room in the house of mirrors that is Moloch. Again, it comes back to the story we enact. The story of Moloch naturally creates conditions that necessitate control. It creates a reality where life is a struggle to survive, and then in order to ensure survival, we must follow the law of Moloch to wherever it leads. We believe we are progressing but never ask what it is that we are progressing towards. Technique has long since passed beyond the barriers of human control. It is an independent force that man can no longer disengage himself from, for man no longer uses Technique; rather, Technique uses man.

Many residents will object, believing that Technique has good, and not evil, as its intent. They see man trying to orient his pursuits around the positive and not the negative. His goal is to create reliable and safe sources of energy. Man develops medicines to heal. He creates entertainment for much needed leisure. He invents machines to reach the stars.

Our technical reality has shown that this is an illusion, because Technique evolves on its own and pursues no end other than itself. Its existing elements combine with new elements, creating newer elements that combine with other existing elements, setting itself on an autonomous course with consequences that cannot be foreseen.

Technique takes man's desire for energy and turns it into nuclear weapons. It takes his medicine for healing and turns it into chemicals for destruction. It takes his entertainment for leisure and creates automatons who can no longer look up. Finally, Technique takes man's machines that were meant to reach the stars and uses them to obscure contact with those very stars through refracted light and electromagnetic pollution.

To grasp the complex phenomenon of Technique and to understand how it is the law of Moloch, is to understand that it is never neutral. Believing otherwise is simply Moloch thinking, a deceptive hubris that echoes throughout our cave environments, "you are still in control, you can master this."

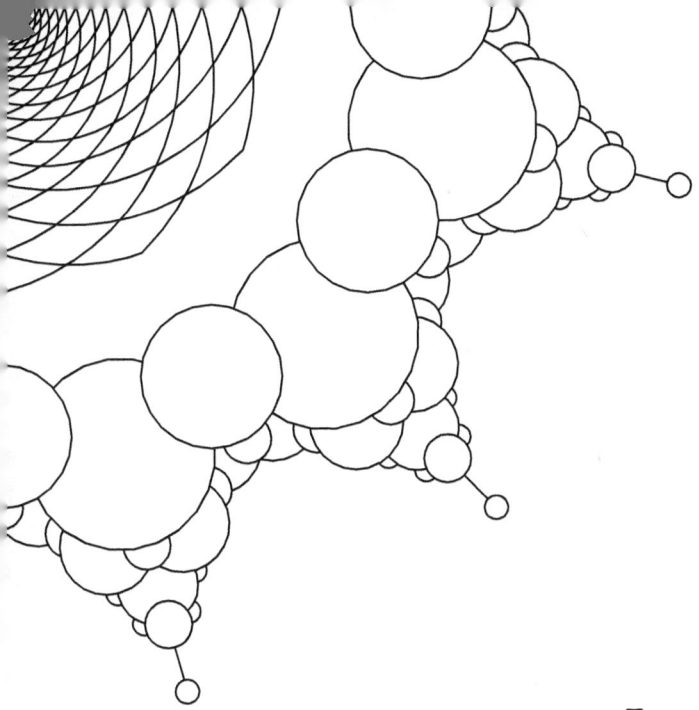

Lesson 21

Sphere of Acquisition

When Moloch is in the mind, it requires the complete submission of its human host to the law of Technique. This law continually structures and directs the thinking of residents so that they are always moving and grasping for the most efficient ways to acquire more. Desire that is overly centered on the self creates artificial needs, and the more needs that a resident has, the more impoverished they become. Poverty is welcome within the halls of Moloch, as it will encourage residents to go deeper into Moloch's many structures.

Moloch is a subtle force that, over time, has the power to create needs where none previously existed. There was a time in the distant past when nature provided everything that humans needed. However, when Moloch entered the mind, humans began to see themselves as separate from the natural world and started obsessing about ways to control nature. As the story of Moloch continued to grow within, our actions, directed by Moloch thinking, began creating an external world that mirrored the internal world of Moloch.

With the inception of Moloch thinking the physical world began to change. Artificial boundaries started dividing and sectioning off the land. Forests were being leveled and turned into money. Agriculture started clearing more land and providing inexpensive food. Man began to congregate in heavily populated areas. Knowledge of plants and wise ways of living were disappearing. Human population started to explode. Man, guided by Moloch thinking and its laws, began his rapid descent out of nature.

Eventually, Moloch thinking directed man to create a civilization where desire promised to fulfill anything that he wanted – control, profits, food, shelter, security, objects and distractions. But with Moloch there is always a price to pay. What is most important must be put to the flames, and only then will Moloch impart to you its power.

If residents wanted to acquire the products of desire, they had to be willing to put their time, talents and energy into Moloch's hands. In exchange for a lifetime of servitude, Moloch would not only provide the basic necessities, but, it would also offer man the illusion of heaven – the ability to have it all. It did this by creating a new concept called work.

Work is birthed out of money. Money, being the object of worship for the residents of Moloch, naturally becomes the focus of desire. If residents wish to have access to money, and by extension, all the needs that money promises to fulfill, then they must work for it, spending their life in pursuit of it. This mental city, being the crafty force that it is, then takes these human gifts of servitude and uses them to further actualize disproportion, imbalance and instability into physical reality.

With Moloch thinking firmly planted within, work naturally served to focus man's attention on what his sacrifice of time would give him in the short term, while completely obscuring what it would take away from him in the long term. Moloch created a reality where life became a struggle to survive. In order to ensure survival, man was compelled to put his faith in Moloch thinking, for it promised him what he so desired. Moloch impoverished man by offering to fulfill his basic needs while simultaneously hiding the fact that his needs would only increase.

Poverty is the presence of many wants. As man's desire for more grew, so did his poverty. Moloch successfully created poverty and then offered up work as the solution for poverty. Trapped within this mental prison, man unknowingly sacrificed all of his time, energy and talents to the creation and actualization of a machine that would do to him what he had done to others. Like his domesticated animals, it was not long before man also came to be seen as a mere object to be exploited, an unfeeling mechanical unit enlisted into the production of more.

Work may seem like a voluntary system, but it is not. When wants are created through the growing materialization of Moloch thinking, a force is unleashed that compels man to participate in a form of compulsory slavery. He is compelled to participate because the necessary relationship that he once had with nature has become lost. He no longer remembers how to live free, as he only knows the cage.

As work evolved and became more efficient, residents were slowly molded into a replaceable mechanical unit within a much larger technical machine of their own making. Work has progressed to the point that, at present, it rarely requires man to think. His only requirement is to follow instructions and to push buttons. Man is the main source of error in technical operations, and the law of Moloch dictates that the source of error must always be eliminated for the sake of efficiency. Thus, man's tasks have been made simple for him through specialization and standardization. He has naturally come to see this as a rational system that guarantees him standardized products that ensure control, safety and security.

In seeing only what this system gives him, man has become blind to the basic human qualities that this mechanization takes away from him. When any being is made to follow dry procedures, and is cut off from creativity, spontaneous free thought, feelings, intuition, responsibility, and free movement, he will become like the machine that he is serving. This is one of the very goals of Moloch: to mechanize and assimilate man into its image so that he will attain a state of unconsciousness, an inert life devoid of any higher thought, so well-conditioned that simply the perception of a real life will suffice. Man will only be defined by his veneers, proudly proclaiming through the halls of Moloch, "I am a systems manager," "I am bureaucrat," "I am a lawyer."

The reality that is created when man is increasingly thrust into evolving systems that do not allow him the ability to act on his own, is a reality in which man can only act as a slave would. If he wishes to not participate, he will be denied money, which essentially means, in Moloch thinking, that he will be punished with starvation and death. Compelled to participate with such a threat to his survival and having no other story to enact, man naturally transforms himself into the needs of the machine and suffers any form of humiliation and degradation, going anywhere and jeopardizing anything to attain more. With obedience to his disinterested labor, he dons a smile and is quick to follow orders, ever eager to please, laboring for that which cannot fill.

In our efforts to control and fulfill our desire for more, we have enacted a story that actually increases our poverty, compelling us to be slaves to a system that has come to exert a monopoly on every area of our life. As our actions become more efficient at placing our part out of balance with the community of life, we can be assured that our problems will only increase. It is here that Moloch will naturally feed us stronger deceptions: if we just work harder and build larger we will get there – if we just had a little bit more money, things would be better.

These illusions have been growing throughout this particular down swing of history, repeating to us that if we could just make it a little bit higher on the pyramid of life, we will make it to heaven. In enacting the story of Moloch, we cannot help but try to climb higher, as this pyramid of success is obsessed with strategies to maintain control. Residents at the bottom of this pyramid are obsessed with finding ways to climb higher, while residents at the top of this pyramid are obsessed with finding ways to maintain control over the masses below.

Man remains trapped in Moloch's environments because he still believes in a story that is creating the problems that he thinks it is fixing. Man does not see that his desire for more, at every step, is further encroaching on his freedom, producing a majority of mechanical slaves and a very small minority of governors to rule over these slaves.

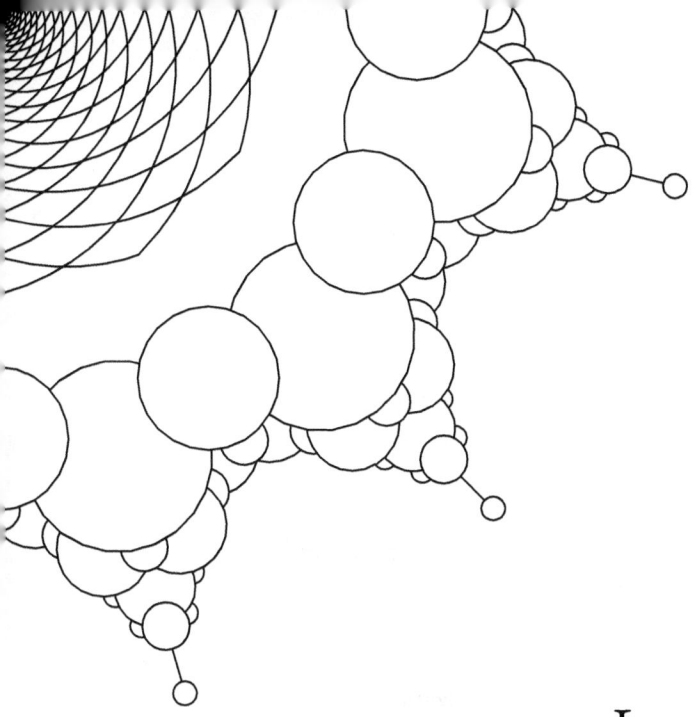

Lesson 34

Sphere of Governance

As our actions, guided by Technique, converted more of the world into ownable objects, a new system was created to protect the ill-gotten gains that we had taken. This system is called government, a product of our desire for safety and security that serves to surround us with another sphere of our own making.

Government, much like the money it protects, is a system of belief. This system materializes and becomes real the more it is believed in. Government is another piece of the unconscious story that we enslave ourselves to. It is a mere social agreement between people that states that man has rights to protect what he has taken. These organizational creations are not a natural phenomenon; rather, they are the playing of roles, the enacting of that same story of control.

It is through the mass belief in government that this idea comes to be endowed with authority. Authority allows government to create laws – laws that are nothing more than the application of force to ensure control. As long as belief in government is maintained by a sufficient number of beings, it will indeed possess a real and tangible power that is able to enforce and legitimize its own existence and boundaries. To be consumed with the pursuit of owning and protecting things is to be blind to the realization that we are ultimately the ones who have come to be owned.

Government is no different than any other action guided by Technique, as it undoubtedly directs itself towards improved means of control. With increasing control comes increasing action that, eventually, fans out to create an unmeasurable web of action and reaction, spawning new problems and new solutions. At present, the law of Moloch has taken a simple idea for attaining safety and security and turned it into an incredibly powerful and expanding force.

Control could produce nothing less, because even simple desires like safety and security will naturally progress to the point where men are hired to physically protect various things. This class of enforcers leads to the creation of a military that is physically able to protect more things. Every new action, in its pursuit of more efficient control, will, by design, create even more actions. With the development of a physical force, like the military, technologies to increase its efficiency will develop.

Spears become arrows, arrows become swords, swords become catapults, catapults become cannons, cannons become rifles, rifles become machine guns, machine guns become tanks, tanks become battleships, battleships become rocket ships, rocket ships become nuclear weapons, and nuclear weapons become drone armies. With each technological step, efficiency is gained, but efficiency comes with a price.

As technologies increase they cannot help but foster and perpetuate even more action. Increasing technological capabilities gives birth to new action, such as intelligence gathering organizations that learn and evolve, gathering more and more data in their quest for safety and security. As this technical organism grows, so does its need for revenue and resources, causing more action such as the increase in taxation and tax enforcing agencies, the continued colonization of new people groups to further expand the debt based systems and the constant creation of profitable wars that serve to create enemies where none previously existed.

The law of Moloch, in its quest for growth and efficiency, produces the same effect on government as it does with everything that it touches. Government, can do no more than become an enormous autonomous technical organism that is beyond the control of those who think they are controlling it. As it grows, it comes to legitimize its own existence. Who could protest the complex body of laws and regulations needed for the dangerous technical applications that have developed from harnessing the power of the atom?

As new technologies and their applications increase, there will always be more laws and regulations to encompass every possible situation that could arise. With these new laws and regulations there comes the increase of law enforcement agencies in order to enforce the new laws and regulations. Residents rarely protest, for who could be against the actions of a police force to ensure less criminals?

Even with the action of law enforcement, the law of Moloch is still at work, making the process of apprehending criminals more efficient, which eventually evolves so as to supervise everyone, knowing exactly what each citizen does, who he knows and how he is entertained. Technical perfection comes through total control. As we develop a world full of complex, vulnerable and powerful technologies, we are obligated to try and anticipate everything in every area. The law of Moloch paves the way to worldwide control.

With expanding control comes expanding complexity. Complexity serves to bewilder the residents of Moloch who naturally group together in various herds. Moloch knows very well that bewildered herds need to be led. Otherwise, like small children, they will trample and destroy everything that Moloch thinking has built. Moloch, therefore, graciously produces a ruling class who excel at its form of thinking. It is this priesthood who mediates the complexities of Moloch to the bewildered masses below them.

It should be understood that, because Moloch thinking is pyramidal, there will always be a small percentage of residents at the top who possess power and wealth and a very large percentage at the bottom who do not. The residents who excel at Moloch thinking have been given the power to present the laity below them with a hand that the masses can see and comprehend, a government of the people, by the people and for the people. However, there is a perverse and ruthless hand that the people are not allowed to see. This hidden hand is the true priesthood, the unbridled story of Moloch, giving real teeth behind the spectacle of government.

In a similar way that a slave has a function on a plantation, so too does the bewildered herd have a function in government. They, like the slave, are merely spectators in the management of the plantation – spectators who are restricted in their movements by taxation and national passports. Unlike the plantation slave, this enslavement is much more insidious as the slave buys into his own slavery. He does not know that he is a slave. Instead, he believes he has an active role in his government, that he has constitutional rights and that he is a liberated human being. Yet, his role and his rights are nothing more than empty privileges granted to him by his masters, a mass illusion fostered to maintain his conformity. This illusion extends to the occasional interest he is shown, as if he were a special type of man, called a voter, who is given the promise of choosing a new plantation master every so many years. This process is most often called an election.

As the various groupings within the herd bicker over which master will hold the whip, the outcome is always controlled. This is because elections are merely bread and circus, keeping the slave distracted through effectual participation, the pushing of buttons or pulling of levers every so many years. These are the very things residents have learned to do so well.

The choice between masters is really no different from the choice prisoners have had to make between two different pieces of paper with different colors, thinking that if they could just choose the right one, their life could be saved. Naturally, the prisoners try hard to make the most meaningful choice, but in reality, the color makes no difference, as it was designed to simply divert their attention away from a system that was exploiting them. Ultimately it serves to put the responsibility on the prisoners, convincing them that it was their fault that they chose the wrong color. By design, this illusion fulfills their desire for importance, control and problem solving, reinforcing the myth that governance can one day solve all of their problems. By their very participation, they give sanction to a coercive and destructive system.

Control over residents spawns the creation of new actions like psychological manipulation, propaganda and the administration of fear. Fear is the perfect motivator for action and it naturally focuses on the herd's desire for self-preservation. If the herd is not properly frightened of all kinds of evil that could destroy them, they may start to see things differently.

To avoid this, the masses are offered a strong image of paradise that promises them safety and security through the destruction of their enemies. Naturally the herd moves quickly to strike down any foe standing between them and this illusion, all to the delight of those who profit from these deceptions. Whether savage, heretic, communist, socialist or terrorist, there exists a long line of titles that can be paraded out to give justification for more control.

In order to properly administer fear and wants to the masses, new actions, called propaganda, were created. This action was easy to implement by those at the top of Moloch's pyramid since they had the money to easily acquire control over new technologies and their communication channels. With this new power, it was an easy matter to seed the masses with vacuous slogans like 'support our troops' or to seed ideas like wearing colored ribbons to show support for varying ideas. These slogans and ideas were constructed in such a way that nobody could really be against them. This is the power of propaganda, as it blinds people to the fact that slogans like 'support our troops' really mean 'support the spheres of Moloch.'

Although the residents who reside at the top of Moloch's pyramid sit in a real seat of power that allows them to mold minds and manipulate opinions, they are not the true puppet masters pulling the strings. These controllers are as much a slave to Moloch thinking as the minds they mold, having little choice but to pull strings, to stir fear and to start endless wars. The same Moloch thinking that motivates the bewildered herd to be continually distracted by their own illusions of climbing the pyramid of control, also motivates those at the top to be continually distracted by their own illusions of maintaining and increasing their control.

Ultimately, it is belief in this story that makes us unseen servants to an enormous technical organism that appears unstoppable. We participate because we cannot see beyond the cave-like environments that Moloch has created. As we have seen, tools created to help the user, quickly through increased efficiency, end up drawing the user under the control of the tool. The tool no longer becomes a means that is serving an end; rather, it becomes the end that must be served because of how it has altered the natural, social and psychological environments in which it has risen.

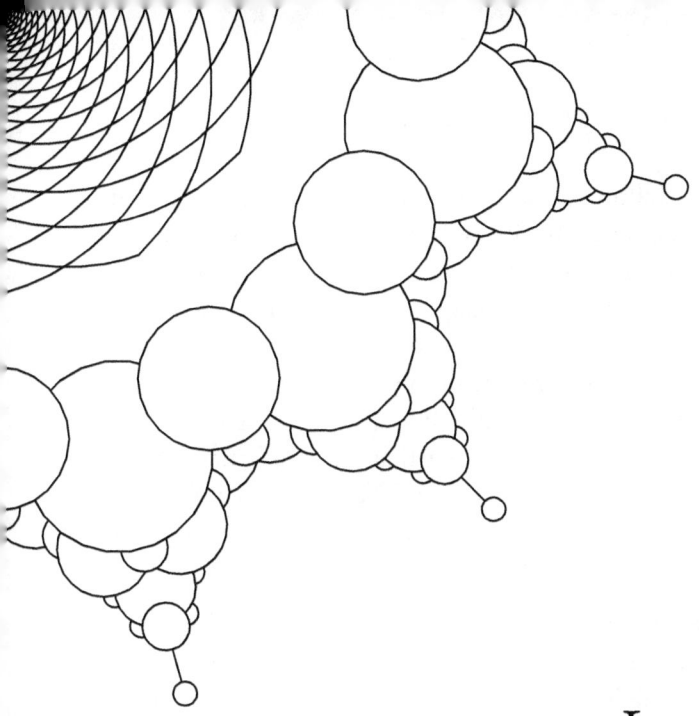

Lesson 55

Sphere of Distraction

In order for a slave to be unaware of his enslavement, he must be made to possess a severely distracted state of awareness. Moloch thinking developed this distracted state through a new action called noise. It is this action that serves to surround man with another sphere of his own creation.

Be still and observe all the screens that surround you. There are screens held in hands, placed over eyes and attached to bodies. They are in work environments, travel environments, home environments and play environments.

They are on billboards, at filling stations, grocery stores and in restaurants. They are in exercise facilities, entertainment facilities, religious facilities and educational environments. Man, now created in the image of Moloch, is a distracted man whose awareness has come to be shaped by the screen, which in its broadest sense, is simply noise. This noise serves to make him content with his artificial surroundings, blinding him to the real structures that are quietly being built around him. Within the realm of Moloch, what is most important, is that residents never be left to themselves, not even for a moment.

The opposite of noise is silence. The city of Moloch is dreadfully afraid of silence, as this non-activity invites the sprouting of higher qualities like reflection, contemplation and meditation – the very things opposed to distraction. Silence is much too frightening to be left to its own devices, and with no other story to enact, man naturally desires a distraction, allowing Moloch to quietly whisper to him "now this."

Before man could even turn his head to notice the silence, a feast of mesmerizing delights appears before him – a virtual reality of distractions. Modern man has come to happily embrace the imposition of noise, barely able to catch his breath between bites, never allowing his eyes or his ears to rest. This feast of noise, whether in the foreground or in the background, has become available anytime and anywhere, having moved into all domains of his life, to such an extent that man is no longer even consciously aware of this noise. He is not aware because he has become the noise, daily inventing new ways to increase the level of noise for himself and for others.

It is important to note that this noise, these activities to occupy our attention, are not normally consumed with some higher goal in mind; rather, they are mostly directed at everything that is pleasurably unessential. Certainly there can be useful and essential information contained within this environment that could ultimately lead a resident to an awareness of its artificial constructs. The city of Moloch is not concerned with this, as it understands that any useful signal can easily be lost in noise. The noise that drowns out useful information is useless information, disconnected facts that have no use other than our own amusement.

The citizens of Moloch believe themselves to be informed, to know something, but they cannot see how small the picture of their knowing is, having been led away by superficial, irrelevant and fragmented information that has been divorced from any real meaning or purpose. Moloch captures our attention only to scatter it, stuffing us full of little picture information that keeps us from experiencing wisdom and understanding within a larger context.

Noise is not inert. It serves a vital purpose within the halls of Moloch, which is to control by shaping and directing individuals. The collective attention of human beings is another form of capital, a commons like the air we breathe or the land underneath our feet that can easily be exploited to further perpetuate that story of separation and control. This brings us back to the action called propaganda. This action is a teacher within the realm of Moloch whose specialty is psychological manipulation – the transformation of free thought into cave reasoning.

The purpose of psychological manipulation is to adapt and integrate man into his environment. Its goal is to mold his tastes, control his thoughts, suggest ideas and produce artificial needs and artificial solutions to those needs, assuaging his hunger for more. Psychological manipulation is an essential requirement of any system that needs constant growth and wealth expansion for its own sustainability. In order to grow, there must be a continual expansion of resources. Continuous expansion means overproduction, which necessitates the creation of new markets.

This is where propaganda comes in to stimulate the appetite by manipulating human desires and wishes. It convinces the population to equate the consumption and accumulation of things with success and happiness. The entire system cannot simply meet human needs but must impose its own needs upon the human, creating consumers who define the value of their existence upon their ability to consume.

To accomplish this, residents must become hooked from birth to highly addictive programming that feeds them the ideology of Moloch. Our brainwaves become manipulated to make consumers of us, keeping us in a mentally infantile state throughout our entire development.

In order to produce this continual state, the screen has developed into a very efficient technology that is able to maintain the eyes of those who submit to its presence. Every few seconds it brings forth a new image, so that the eye never rests, always with something new to see.

This unseen mechanism for conditioning has been so effective, in part, because of a willing society that has unquestioningly allowed this new teacher into almost every home, in almost every country and in almost every class. Our physical spaces have been reoriented around this device, literally perched like an idol in the center of the home with everything facing it. In essence, the staring in reverential attention to the images and sounds that emanate from this digital idol have become so important that, apart from sleeping, there is no other activity that occupies so much of a resident's time. It has become the surrogate influencer, parent and teacher to the residents of Moloch, often operating out of a room that is called living.

By focusing one's attention onto a screen, the propagandee becomes voluntarily complicit by inserting himself into a psychological and behavioral modification structure that compels him to buy into collective motivations. This new reality tunnel teaches him a specific set of artificial constructs and deceptive illusions called small picture values, which are purely immersed in Moloch thinking. These values are absorbed and integrated into one's life, so much so that life becomes directed by them.

The power of the screen even reaches those residents who try to limit their exposure to it. If the screen cannot get man, then all those who live by the message of the screen will propagandize him. This occurs through every interaction of his daily life, as each consumer of the screen easily becomes an unwitting salesperson, displaying, promoting, living and working with propaganda. In this way, propaganda rarely leaves any gaps. It is continuous and lasting, creating imperceptible influences that are constantly reinforced through repetition.

One of the greatest lessons that propaganda teaches is mere consumption – the glorification of consuming images, information, products, packages and personalities. It is a lesson that educates all residents into the acquisitive value system, producing a never ending orgy of consumption. The message is clear: our cultural values, self-worth, quality of life and happiness are measured by the ownership and consumption of things, a life whose philosophy is accumulation.

Propaganda teaches its lesson through the daily parade of fabricated spectacles and products that light up our screens. This artificial environment serves to shift our focus away from higher things by surrounding us with a fog of shallow materialism, creating a life that has been reduced to simply projecting an image, an image that we become the servant to.

Still, we love our propaganda as it promises what we desire: happiness, health, beauty and success. Our happiness, health, beauty and success appear to be the paramount values of the screen, suggesting that we can have it all simply by increasing our consumption. This message is powerful, as every product is turned into a symbol that appears to satisfy our deep needs, taking away fear and creating a new man by their mere acquisition. To pursue these products is to pursue the artificial meanings attached to these products. The longer we are immersed in such symbol manipulation, the more we cling to stereotyped notions. We have evolved beyond being the consumer to becoming the product being sold. All of this is a continuation of psychological conditioning that is solely focused on the creation of needs and the fabrication of wants.

This is one reason celebrities hold the gaze of so many. A celebrity, too, is an image – a symbol of happiness, health and success, living in the promised land of complete and total consumption. We tend to know more about people on the screen than we do about people in real life, as we daily absorb this fictitious community that is presented to us, the spectator. We do not see the celebrity for what they really are – a commodity in the form of a caricature, created, molded and shaped to teach and buttress the conception of life within our mental environments. Unfortunately, they are most often seen as a human who eventually made it to the Promised Land, just like we will someday. To be a celebrity to the masses and to be celebrated by the masses is not something that comes forth naturally; rather, it is something that must be wedded to powerful institutions who are able to disseminate an artificial image to the masses.

Ultimately, the screen helps to create a mass citizen who can only see with their physical eyes. He cannot feel but only reacts. He is reduced to the most useful pattern of his particular society – an inert individual who only becomes active when he is set in motion. Instead of anxiety and confusion, propaganda has given him certainty. When propaganda stops, anxiety appears.

Though man has long been propagandized, he also becomes a propagandist, following trends, branding himself, wearing what he is told to wear, driving what he is told to drive, watching what he is told to watch, behaving how he is told to behave and eating what he is told to eat. Man has become puerile and intellectually inert. In this state there is no reason to limit access to information and no reason to conceal the truth; rather, there is every reason to widen access so that any piece of truth that may emerge can be drowned in a sea of irrelevance.

To exist behind this digitized veil is to be prevented from touching a new reality. It is to give power over to storytellers, the keepers of the gate, the senders that Moloch has bred. In this unconscious act, we no longer become the storytellers. Instead, we have handed this function over to professionals who create an environment that sets the limits of our reality. This is done by classifying, framing, reducing, enlarging, coloring and sequencing an argument for a reality made in the image of Moloch.

We hide behind this veil because we know no other world. The limits of the veil have become the limits of our perception. This veil, though, is by no means oppressive; rather, it feels quite natural due to the steady stream of ideas and information that conform to our upbringing within the boundaries of Moloch. Already familiar to us, these sounds and images solidify our confidence in this framework, reinforcing our belief in the story of Moloch.

One mass illusion propagated by the digitized veil of Moloch is that we are existing within a stream of society that is striving towards a new and more perfect world. This new heaven maintains our focus away from our narrow environments, away from the veil and away from the darkness beyond. Here in our seats, we are convinced that we are going somewhere, and not alone, but with all those who are seated around us – those who hear and see what we hear and see.

When Moloch is in the mind, it creates residents who are compelled to act as seduced pawns, freely submitting to a system that exploits them for their attention, energy and existence. Pawns, within this system, are more interested in reacting to the game they find themselves in, convinced that they are the users of this game rather than the ones being used. Instead of searching for understanding as to the purpose of this game, they maintain their attention within a fixed set of boundaries and rules. In this atrophied state, they are unable and unwilling to envision anything bigger, afraid of what they might find if they were to get off the board and start bumping around in the dark.

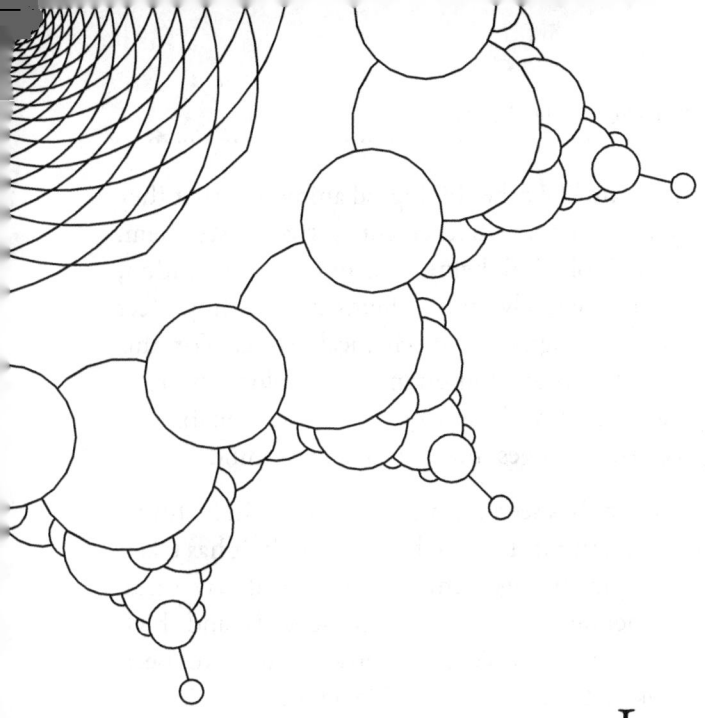

Lesson 89

Sphere of Indoctrination

Moloch thinking is desire trapped within a small view of self. Selfish desire produces actions that know no end. These actions not only create voluntary systems like the screen, that mold minds into Moloch's many spheres, but they also go so far as to create mandatory systems that require Moloch's youngest members be trained in this art of pursuing more. This sphere of indoctrination is a mandatory system of schools that Moloch has developed to enforce, by law, the shaping of perception, blotting up any attention spared by the screen.

Humans are like other biological animals in that they will naturally bond with whatever entity that raises them. Whether it is a biological being, machine or institution, children will unknowingly mold themselves with perfect docility to these biological or mechanical hands. For this reason, it was of the utmost importance for Moloch thinking to develop an additional sphere that was capable of converting even the youngest minds into a mass mind.

This sphere has seen a gradual evolution in its forms and methods throughout the ages, but at present, it has taken the form of simple management systems called day cares, preschools, elementary schools, middle schools and high schools. And for those residents whose wills have been sufficiently broken to qualify for a higher position in this system of more, there are also colleges, universities, seminaries and graduate schools.

Any system based on control needs to be labeled, measured, graded, standardized and quantified. To achieve this, schools naturally mirror the processes of a factory, as they both come from the same thinking. Like the factory, children are simply raw products who are shaped and fashioned into standardized products that are predictable and controllable. They must be made to conform and be as alike as possible so that they will be well adapted to their role in Moloch's labor force of mechanization and exploitation.

Like the factory, human products are regulated centrally by the application of formulas – specifications imposed by experts called national standards. Within this system, human qualities such as creativity, curiosity, intuition, reflection and contemplation are not very useful. However, being competitive, punctual, obeying authority, being classified and graded, moving at the sound of a bell and enduring long hours of mundane and repetitive work are very useful. Just like the factory, those who excel at this joyful serfdom will gladly receive graded promotions from their superiors.

To mold young minds into Moloch's way of thinking is simply a matter of control. It starts with mandatory confinement during most of the early years of a child's life. This confinement serves to separate children from the immense diversity of life by plunging them into a monocultural setting that surrounds them with other students who are of the same age and social class. In this confinement, there is almost always a precise regulation of a student's time, usually administered by a bell that has the power to start and stop student's activity – activities that include having children think about the same things at the same time and in the same ways.

By controlling the environment, a total claim can be made to the time and energies of those confined within these walls. This claim is made by the teachers who become the sole custodian, disciplinarian, authority, therapist and priest. The teacher is essentially the master of ceremonies who will guide their students through daily rituals in order to shape and mold them into products worthy of Moloch's many spheres.

It should not be surprising that teachers are products of this same compulsory system. By the very act of teaching within this system, they have placed themselves in a more rigid structure than that imposed upon the children. As products from the same manufacturing system, teachers are enforcers of bureaucratic rules, quietly managing a continual project that has ongoing consequences for themselves and for the students they believe they are teaching.

Teachers are the perfect enforcers. If a corporation or government were to be seen as the ones controlling the knowledge that could be imparted, there would most certainly be an outcry of indignation, of censorship and of indoctrination. However, when learning is directed by teachers, the controlling of knowledge is welcomed. Knowledge, within Moloch's educational environments, has to be controlled. Whoever governs the educational systems will naturally provide endless lessons about itself, on the virtuousness of its own history, on the wisdom of its own economic systems and on those lessons that serve to highlight the hardships, abuse and anarchy that once reigned before its arrival.

These educational rituals are not inert, as they have been crafted with great care by a central command of Moloch thinkers called social engineers. These engineers develop institutionally planned lessons that package meanings and values into instruction manuals that are labeled 'curriculum.' This is Moloch thinking at work, as sources of information must be organized, limited and applied with discrimination. The flow of information must be controlled, broken down into courses, subjects and fields of study. Priority must always be given to that which best creates students with Moloch in their minds

Education under Moloch thinking is an information management program that categorizes and highlights what is legitimate knowledge, all the while systematically excluding, demeaning and labeling as trivial, that which the management program deems as illegitimate knowledge – that which is outside the cave environments. Each year, students are compelled to consume these programs until they are replaced with a new offering the next school year. These systems use the teacher as the distributor to deliver the product to the consumer, whose responses and reactions will be studied and used to make more potent versions of the same material so as to improve efficiency.

The sphere of education is so complete that even if there are some students who do not adapt themselves well to this confinement and its rituals, then Moloch has provided a guidance counselor, someone tasked with helping the student adapt to his environment. If a student continues to prove unadaptable then there are chemical controls implemented, called medication. Beyond these measures, if, by chance, there are parents who do not wish to go along with these indoctrinating rituals administered by strangers, there is the backing of law and police power to help enforce the mandatory filling of these seats.

It is rare that these measures are needed, as the myth of schooling is incredibly powerful. Through its doors lie the promise of salvation. Outside its doors lies damnation. The promise of salvation is simply that a good education will mean a good job. A good job means good money. Good money brings pure happiness. Damnation is simply the belief that the under consumption of school leads to a bad job with low pay. Low pay brings pain, struggle and hardship. Those within the doors of this church are a captive audience learning from their priests what is right and wrong, daily shaping their vision of truth to match what is being taught. Inevitably, such instruction produces students who internalize the greatest lesson of school: the unspeakable naturally becomes unthinkable.

The myth of school is another form of the Faustian bargain; that on the hopes of some future gain, one must surrender their present humanity. What is left are automatons – souls that have lost the desire to grow, only knowing the need to be taught – souls whose needs for affirmation are mediated by the pursuit of an A average – souls whose inner life have been subordinated, only knowing how to walk on prescribed paths and follow prescribed customs. Moloch does not have to worry about putting these citizens into their places since they will do it voluntarily, squeezing themselves into any available niche that they have been taught to seek.

A successful graduate of mandatory schooling is well versed in Moloch thinking, ready to be immersed in its mechanical world. He may be able to read, but he has trouble reflecting on what he reads. He knows numbers as quantities he can use to compete and manipulate the physical world, but he knows very little about their symbolic, philosophical and spiritual character. He knows the science of a small mechanical world, but he knows very little about mystery, reverence and awe. He knows how to race, to compete and to win, to finish life with more points than his opponents, having participated in his school's structured sports programs; however, he does not know how to enjoy the journey, how to play with improvisation and spontaneity for no other reason than for enjoyment. He knows how to permanently label others as low class material and high class material, having been publicly labeled himself with his permanent record of graded promotions; but, he knows very little about interconnectedness. He knows how to consume knowledge, ideas and images of others, but he has a hard time creating his own knowledge, ideas and images. Ultimately, he will be well prepared to enter a competitive life, having no vital interest other than his motivation to find a career, any career, regardless of the subject matter, as long as it ensures him the highest monetary return on his investment of confinement.

At its core, mandatory schooling is a form of thought control that prevents residents from opening their eyes to see through the illusions that have surrounded them. When we learn to give ourselves over to those with power, not talking out of line or asking troublesome questions, we naturally carry this mentality throughout our life, submitting to what our bosses, tax collectors or money surrogates tell us, scared that we might be fired or even be made homeless.

Schooling is one ritual process among many that introduces us to discordant forces that shape our world, keeping us unquestionably serving the spheres that surround us. This spell cannot be broken if we remain unconscious about these systems.

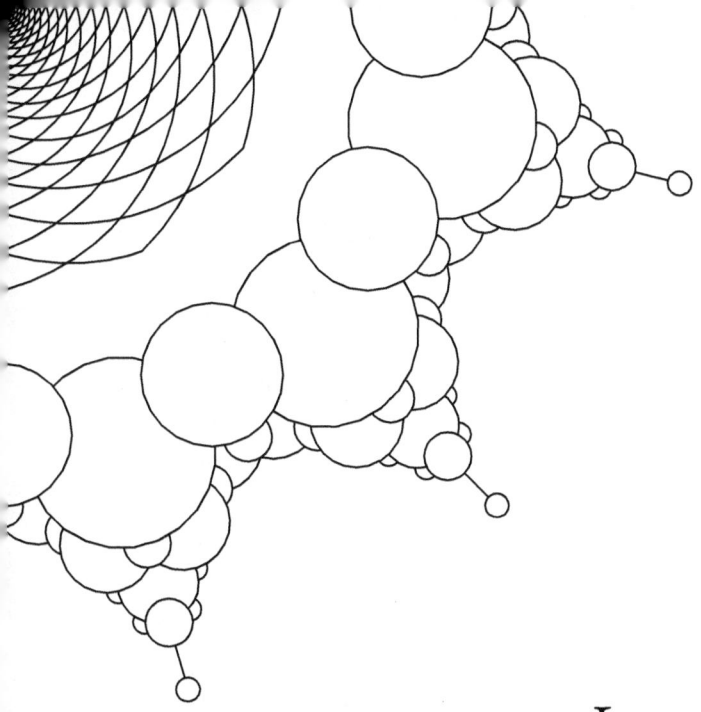

Lesson 144

Building Blocks of Language

It is at this point that we must again step back in order to examine the phenomena of language; the very building blocks of this mental city. Language is made up of a collection of symbols – signs that can be made present to our senses and imagination that aid us in communication. Though often unseen, these symbols wield an enormous power over reality.

When picking currants, we naturally change our perspective. We bend down, shift to the right, then to the left and move around within the plant. We know, intuitively, that if we just stood in one fixed position, even though we would certainly pick quite a few berries, we would be missing out on so many more berries hidden within, blocked by the many leaves. Language is often like the leaves. Our fixed position is our conditioning and the berries are simply the experience.

Language, like leaves, are important. Without language, it would be difficult to fully create an experience. From a fixed position, language will certainly show us many good and beneficial things, but it will also hide many more good and beneficial things. It does not do this on purpose, being intentionally deceptive; rather, it cannot help but limit what can be seen due to its necessary structure.

These limits, which are built into language, naturally become the limits of our reality. Though unintentional, limits can be deceptive, as they are able to reduce our awareness to merely surface things. These perceivable surfaces tend to create a belief in the totality of their perspective. To exist in a state that is unaware of the power that language wields over reality is to be equally unaware of the material used to create our cave-like environments – the building blocks of language.

The danger with language is forgetting that symbols are parts within a process. These parts are always pointing to something beyond themselves. Symbols, by their very nature, are not the thing symbolized. Symbols are like a map that is pointing to a territory. Maps are separated from the territory they point to, being only a crude approximation of it.

Symbols are incapable of conveying the whole truth of reality.

Language is a second order phenomena, a verbal world that exists because it is reflecting and pointing to an experiential world. This verbal world is a crude abstraction, an approximation that captures only a small aspect of its referent. As second order phenomena, symbols are not natural but cultural. They are not instinctive but learned. Our learned languages are an unconscious system that creates a fixed way of interpreting our experience, like grooves that our thoughts naturally slide into. The danger lies in seeing and hearing only what the grammatical constructs of our language have made us sensitive to, believing that our reduced awareness is the only awareness.

Language is Moloch's specialty. Reality within the city of Moloch is not permitted to come to us unnamed or unadorned; rather, it must be draped in the cultural prejudices of language. These prejudices are powerful because they are capable of guiding our thoughts towards normative ends, comforting us with familiar categories. Naturally, we become so deeply immersed within our own linguistic assumptions that we become incapable of recognizing a truer reality, simply because it does not come to us in its proper clothing. Essentially, this means that our perception of what is, is most often governed by what we already believe to be there. To approach the process alone, moving beyond the adornments of language, is something that we have forgotten how to do.

Our fixed perceptions, within a world of words, is the very thing that stands between us and a more expansive reality. These words keep us fixed within our cave-like environments, on the small subset of reality that these words have illuminated. The fact that others seated with us perceive the same things reinforces this perception, creating love lines that tether us to these artificial environments, drawing us into a conformity that sees our perspective as the most real and authentic form of reality. We have become so deeply entrenched within our own linguistic assumptions that we are prevented from seeing that our reality is almost entirely based upon the cave environments that we were born into.

Cave environments are the stories surrounding us. Once a story is established, we develop an incredible ability to delete information that does not support this story, as well as an amazing capacity to only search out information that confirms it. Within our cave environments we are taught early on that our codified perceptions are never to be questioned, only defended.

Language is never inert and goes far beyond aiding us in communication. When language is wedded to the self-centered story of Moloch, it gives shape and support to our controlling structures, creating maps we must follow throughout our lives. From birth, we are imprinted with these maps that provide instructions to follow and beliefs to adopt. Naturally, we set ourselves on a course to learn and memorize them. A much larger reality could be all around us, right next to us, staring us in the face and we would not notice it, blinded by the structures that stand between us and a multitude of hidden treasures.

Language is the necessary building material for cave environments. To use language is to categorize, abstract, label and represent the world through symbols that involuntarily divide up the world into separate objects that are to be acted upon, essentially creating, by its use, a world of 'others.' Language gives primacy to the role of the observer, convincing us that we are separate and able to make distinctions where we please. Yet, our distinctions are only capable of highlighting mostly arbitrary things. These distinctions that we create serve to reveal more about where we, the observer, stand in comparison to the world which we are trying to capture.

One example of this is the deception hidden within the verb 'to be.' Agnubi is stupid, trees are solid, the Bible is the Word of God. These are not statements about what things really are. They are surface understandings of how things appear to us from a certain perspective. These words, coupled with the verb 'to be,' really only indicate our limited viewpoint and feelings about something much more complex than symbols could ever describe. Words like stupid, clever, smart and dumb are not characteristics of Agnubi; rather, they are the product of fixed perceptions – surface perceptions of a complex being. These words do not even begin to describe the complex phenomenon of Agnubi; however, since we have spoken them and placed them in this natural world, they become real to us. Agnubi, then, becomes stupid to us. The rest of what Agnubi is becomes lost to us. The same goes for solid and any other grammatical construct that we create.

Nouns, also, in their attempt to solidify a process, force a multitude of mysterious and unique processes into generic finite categories, reducing the diversity and uniqueness of every moment into 'this' or 'that.' Trees, regardless of their uniqueness, intelligence and diversity become simply trees, a solid mass containing material called wood. Having been conditioned to this surface label, our perception of trees prevents us from seeing their uniqueness. Language forces us to see only what its structure creates for us and allows us to see. Like a man trapped in a house, we see the outside world from a fixed position, through windows that hide more than they reveal.

Within the realm of Moloch, our language carries the assumption of control. When we label and categorize the world, we impose our order upon it. In essence, we separate and domesticate it. Not surprisingly, within the generic categories of control is birthed an enormous power to destroy. This can be seen by, again, looking at the abstraction of a dynamic forest into, simply, static trees. Trees, in reality, are not static objects but dynamic life giving processes, a perpetual dance of movement, living interconnected organisms that are constantly changing, growing, transforming and communicating. However, when language takes the complex and reduces it to surface abstractions, they become a simple object to be controlled and exploited for profit. Our language literally creates a reality in which trees are an 'other.' This separated 'other' is easily used in our quest for more. It is not hard to see how an entire region could be deforested without so much as a thought.

What we do to others, we end up doing to ourselves. Through our fixation on symbols, we have effectively facilitated our own exploitation. This is done by creating generic categories for processes found within the world. When language abstracts living processes into simple static terms like slave, savage, immigrants, meat, employee, foreigner, mentally ill, animal, customer, terrorist, primitive or the poor, then abuse, exploitation and destruction come much more easily. Language facilitates the creation of 'others,' and in Moloch's world, 'others' are a category to be acted upon from above.

Language possesses an enormous power to give shape to our world. Its role in the building of Moloch has no parallel. Language, too, must follow the law of Moloch. Language grows and expands, and with every new application of Technique comes new words, new subsets of language, new vocabulary and an infinite spectrum of words defined by each other. Each new level serves to separate and distance us further and further from what they are pointing to.

To worship our inherited symbols is to unknowingly worship the cave-like environments that gave birth to these symbols. Words reflect and defend that which gave birth to them, expressing values and ways of living that form a certain local reality for their user. Their use creates and perpetuates the world from which they came, keeping us trapped in a socially constructed world of our own making that prevents the emergence of other worlds.

We believe, as one under a spell, that our minds are in control of language and that it is simply a vehicle that we use to express. Instead, it is language that rules over our minds – language is the driver. As a resident of Moloch, we unconsciously learn to think like Moloch and codify the stories, beliefs, truths and values of Moloch into every sentence that we speak.

Since we are birthed into a world that Moloch thinking has created in its image, we have become parties to an agreement. Even though this agreement is unspoken, we are, nevertheless, obligated to abide by its terms. Its terms state that, if we are to talk and be understood, then we must subscribe to its organizational structure, to its system of classification and to its verbs and nouns. The question is not if we are parties, which we all are, but rather, are we aware that we are parties? Do we understand what language is doing? Are we conscious of its force in creating our reality? To remain unconscious of its force is to have arrived at our most important stage of conditioning, where the cave becomes all there is and all there ever will be, a complete reality that is really a reduced reality.

The key with language is not to advocate its abolition; rather, it is to be mindful of its relative unreality – being conscious of how we use it and how it uses us – understanding that it is humans who are the creators of these maps. We do no merely inherit stories, we are the story tellers.

If we wish to truly explore reality, to touch and taste its fruit, we must understand the purpose of language within the context of a much larger and dynamic process. As this much larger picture comes into focus, only then can we begin to see language through the eyes of gratitude, as something that has been pointing the way all along. This is where we discover the silence of experience lying beyond the many symbols. When it becomes necessary to break this silence, to describe its territory with symbols, it will then be done with a conscious awareness of map making, understanding that whatever it is, it is not.

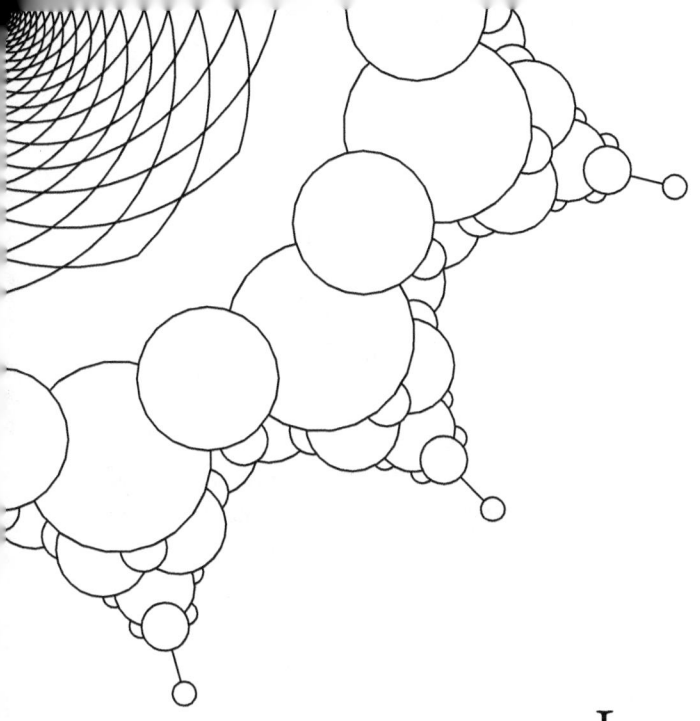

Lesson 233

Sphere of Certainty

Be still and observe. Observe, within you, the innate desire to explore and investigate your existence, to understand your place within this universe. Observe the longings within to reunite and reconnect with that something, that we at times, seem so disconnected from. Though often obscured by our distracted state, it is this deep and natural sense of curiosity that pushes us to grow beyond what we were before.

Moloch, for its part, understands our intrinsic sense of curiosity. For this reason, it goes about transforming this human quality into a static position. Essentially, it creates human belief systems that takes the higher qualities of humility, reverence and awe, and replaces them with the lower qualities of hubris and certainty.

When Moloch is in the mind, our desire to explore often devolves into a desire to know with absolute certainty. This desire produces actions that actualize into reality a new sphere that is designed to give us exactly what we want. Inside these environments, residents are daily convinced that certainty is now theirs, that they now know, and that there could not possibly be any other way. Moloch, indeed, gives certainty, but in exchange for this certainty, it quietly takes away growth.

Within the sphere of certainty there are many different structures that function in very similar ways. At the top of these structures you will almost always find a craft of kings – a ruling class of the scientific experts, educational leaders, religious pundits and intellectual elites who have, throughout the ages, placed themselves in a position as gatekeepers to greater realities. Daily, they pontificate from their cathedrals, universities, institutions, seminaries and churches, proclaiming that truth is only approachable through their methodological framework, through their ideologies, canons and doctrines.

Truth, salvation and enlightenment do not exist outside of their structures, for only foolishness and darkness reside there. If there is a truth that is said to be found outside of this framework, it will be aggressively denied and promptly ridiculed. If there are any who claim to have found this truth, they will quickly be treated as heretics, having rejected the conventional understanding of their community. Within these structures the process of self-directed examination is repressed by the application of fear based conformity.

For the craft of kings, maintaining their structures has become their trade. Maintaining their need for superiority and control has quietly become their profession. Claiming ownership over truth has provided the craft of kings with real power. They have used this power to establish the boundaries of thought. These boundaries hem their masses into well-constructed paths that enforce where inquiry must start and stop. Ultimately, this serves to close their listeners off to any larger realities that surround them.

Throughout the ages, the craft of kings has perfected their message and sold it to an eager audience for a profit. They have gladly accepted payments in exchange for the opportunity to speak about what they know with certainty – filling minds with maps. This craft is not a natural system within reality; rather, it is, and has always been, something we created, as it was our own desire that sought out these producers of certainty and gave them a voice.

Once the priesthood was given a voice, they quickly moved to guard and protect it through the creation of levels – floors that keep a clear distinction between the initiated and the uninitiated. In order to qualify to become a priest in this community, certain initiation rituals must be performed. Indoctrination, in the form of training, must be submitted to by approved institutions. Proper theological, doctrinal and scientific stances must be attained. Proof of these must be submitted, reviewed and approved by peers, who themselves have already submitted their minds to the required methodological frameworks. Memberships and affiliations must be obtained within credible organizations in order to demonstrate a commitment to conformity. When these rituals have been successfully completed, only then can those coveted letters be placed behind a name. Titles like reverend, pastor, priest and pope can then be properly granted. Lab coats and clergy costumes can then be worn. Finally, embossed certificates can then be hung in plain sight, serving as daily reminders of their servitude.

Arriving at this point of prominence within these structures is to lead residents in rituals of symbol worship, which is most often the act of veneration towards a particular sacred map. These maps are the axiomatic systems, scriptures, laws, canons and creeds, providing certainty by directing and guiding the thoughts of residents. Residents come to view these maps as containing the entire domain of truth and as being the only valid way of seeking knowledge. Salvation and truth, they are told, are only found in unquestioning adherence to these maps. Residents naturally obsess over understanding the maps given to them, working harder and harder to arrive at the illusion of a perfect 1:1 map.

In many scientific structures, it is believed that to measure is to know. When something is measured, it is essentially the converting of reality into the language of number. This language is another form of abstraction – another step in reducing the infinite variability of reality into standard and definable parts. To measure is to convert quality into quantity. It is to take process and turn it into structure, to make what is unique into what is uniform and to turn what is dynamic into that which is static. Through better numbering and finer labeling, more sophisticated models develop, better definitions emerge, and new axiomatic systems are created. Ultimately, these systems evolve into sacred maps – the attempt to capture all of reality within their specific formulas. Maps are based and built upon assumptions about the nature of reality, and through these maps, users are compelled to guide their experiences and observations.

Numbers, like words, are powerful. It is through the illusion of these symbols that an enormous and expanding structure has been created that excels at making maps of maps of maps. These structures have become so large and so complex through hyper-specialization that it has become almost completely inaccessible to its residents, constraining its members to work only within their own narrowly accessible part.

Unknowingly, desire has created a massive labyrinth that leads further and further into its infinite center, convincing its residents that because of their hard work at gaining knowledge and interpretation, certainty is now theirs. Blinded by the hubris of being guided solely by the adherence to the tools of science, they have become trapped in a small picture environment that says its laws, theorems and axiomatic systems are the only indisputable source of truth.

Science, in its quest to capture all of reality within a finite set of axioms, laws and rules, cannot help but end in failure as its basis lies in mathematics, in number, or more simply put, in abstraction. No matter how finely detailed a map or model of reality is, regardless of how close science gets to a 1:1 ratio, there will always be something of great value that is missing due to the built in limitations of a static map.

Ultimately, a map created by science must be built upon the tools of science. This map will only be able to reflect what the tools of science are capable of handling. This built in incompleteness is not unknown to its priests; rather, it is simply ignored and treated as if it does not exist. Acknowledging the impossibility of any formal system being able to capture all truths in a finite set of axioms means that the only thing certain is that certainty is not only elusive, but completely unattainable through the tools of science.

Although maps serve a purpose and can be very useful, there are limits to what can be proven. This is the very nature of abstraction, as ultimate reality lies beyond the abstraction and cannot be reached through the worship of a finite collection of axioms. Regardless of the systems man creates, it must be understood that they will always be doomed to incompleteness.

Science, when fueled by the desire for certainty, will continue to take the whole of reality apart, believing that it is only adding strength to what it already knows by isolating, separating and naming the many parts. In essence, science has separated and broken down a book into chapters, paragraphs, sentences, words and letters. The composition of these letters are studied, the ink is analyzed, along with the fibers of the paper. Science believes it knows what this book is. It has, however, missed what this book is about. In taking parts and separating them from process, they possess some understanding, but only of parts in isolation – a reflection of Moloch in their minds. Without realizing it, they have failed to grasp the purpose, spirit and meaning of this ongoing book called life.

To hear, touch and taste the fluid process of reality and to uncover our place within it, requires that we go beyond the tools of science, that we transcend the measuring and the naming. Understanding comes through relationship. It is found in how the letters relate to each other in words, how the words relate to each other in sentences, how sentences relate to paragraphs and how these relate to the whole. We can spend our life making maps and models of what reality is, correcting them, rearranging them, scaling them, trying to make our maps indistinguishable from reality itself. And while this may seem like a worthwhile endeavor within a small picture reality, it is an illusion that will keep us lost in the endless labyrinth of our own cave-like environments.

In many religious structures it is believed that to possess in written word communications from the divine is to know. These words make up their sacred maps – their scriptures, creeds, canons, doctrines and theological stances that desire to capture all truths within their written words. At the heart of these sacred maps is revelation. Revelation is the divine giving of thoughts, words and inspiration to man. The problem comes when revelation is abstracted by writing it down, making it a standardized form from which belief can be derived.

To write is to map the experience of what may have been a real manifestation, making it something less than what it originally was. These maps are not seen as pointing to something that lies beyond verbal description; rather, they are seen as indisputable sources of truth.

Words are powerful. Through the worship of these symbols an enormous and expanding structure has been created that excels at making maps of maps of maps. It has become so large that its numerous floors have become inaccessible to each other, keeping its residents focused only on their own specific doctrinal map. Desire has created a massive labyrinth that can easily lead further and further into its infinite center, convincing its residents that, because of their divine words, their hard work at gaining knowledge, and through more accurate translations and interpretations, certainty has become theirs. Blinded by the hubris of being guided by their sacred maps, residents have become trapped in an environment that repeatedly says there is no need to look any further, as all truths are contained within these narrow environments.

Religion, in its quest to organize truth by capturing the words of God, cannot help but end in failure, as its basis lies in language. When dealing with language, we are dealing with a separation between the symbol and the thing symbolized. Symbols are shared rules connecting a symbol to their meaning. How symbols relate to what is being symbolized is mainly derived from cultural traditions, meaning it is learned and not instinctive.

At its root, a symbol is fundamentally ambiguous. Its meaning can never completely be controlled. Meaning is not found only in the symbols we use, but is also constructed by what the listener or reader interprets them to mean through the filter of their own perspectives. Our interpretation of words that we believe are divine can only be but attempts to approximate, through the sullying influence of time, the intent of their perceived author. In this endeavor, there can never be complete certainty that our approximations equal the intent of the original experience.

When dealing with maps, no matter how hard and how long we work at better translation, interpretation and understanding, and no matter how close we get to a 1:1 map, there will always be something missing due to the limitations built into the map itself. Most of the priesthood is aware of the inherent incompleteness of their maps. Their response is to ignore it and approach their sacred words as if these limitations do not exist, repeating daily that these words are the Word of God, so much so that they become them for their listeners. For the priesthood to acknowledge the impossibility of any formal system being able to capture and organize all truths into a finite set of symbols, means that the only thing certain is that certainty is not only elusive, but completely unattainable through the use of language.

Acknowledging these limitations would mean the end of fundamentalism and the end of seeing sacred texts as the Holy Grail for knowledge of spiritual things. Inherent limitations are the nature of abstraction. Religious maps serve a purpose and can be quiet useful, but it is the worship of them that prevents the emergence of what these words were trying to point to. Regardless of the systems man creates, it must be understood that they cannot help but be doomed to incompleteness.

Religion, when fueled by the desire for certainty, will continue to force reality to fit within their maps. Religion has missed what these words are pointing to by taking the spirit behind these words and forcing them to fit within man made systems of doctrine and theology. The letter will always constrain, focusing our attention on surface things as opposed to the creative movement that gave birth to the letter. We can spend our lives making maps and models of what reality is, correcting them, rearranging them, scaling them and trying to make our maps indistinguishable from reality itself. While it may seem like a worthwhile endeavor, it is an illusion that will keep us lost in another endless labyrinth.

Structures create their own nested hierarchy of stories. Within the sphere of certainty, almost all structures contain a story that explains the workings of the world, answering the questions of why we are here and where we are going. Since the primary value of Moloch is self-centeredness, it should be evident that its stories would ultimately reflect that which gave birth to them, as stories cannot help but illuminate the values of their creator.

Scientific structures contain a story that teaches its residents to be certain about a small picture reality that says that we are simply products of chance, physical creatures whose electrochemical structure somehow functions to produce a state of awareness. These organisms naturally compete in order to survive and pass on their genes. Competition for survival is the basis of natural selection, with life forms competing with each other for resources. Within this story, the deepest purpose of life is to survive and reproduce by whatever means necessary.

Having grown up within the spheres of Moloch, this is not a difficult story to buy into, since almost everywhere we look, life tends to embody the idea of competition. Everything appears to be a struggle to survive. This struggle is seen as a good thing, as competition creates progress in all realms: genetic, economic, evolutionary, technological, educational and many more. To enact this story is to simply out compete, to improve through efficiency, to dominate our competitors.

Through these structures of certainty, Moloch has silently co-opted our desire to explore. It takes this desire and uses it to further extend its own reach. Stories create and guide action. Because of science, new worlds are daily being colonized. Science, having learned how to harness some of the forces of nature, continues to tame the big and the little. With every new small picture understanding and discovery, Moloch promptly exploits it in order to achieve more control. Why should it not? As products of chance, forever on the edge of oblivion, why not control and manipulate nature to better our chances of survival and fulfill the techno-utopians dream for heaven on earth – a place of safety, health and comfort that can only be achieved by overcoming the world and keeping it under our control? As we are soothed by this mythology, we gain knowledge and believe this knowledge to be inert. In Moloch thinking, knowing how to split an atom is simply a scientific discovery, free of value. But, as we have seen, the autonomous law of Moloch respects nothing, showing us only what it will do for us and hiding what it will undo.

Stories produce consequences. One of the consequences within the sphere of certainty is that our perspective becomes trapped. The limits of our perspective will always define the limits of our reality. To exist within a structure that teaches us that the world is simply material and that chance, plus unending time, produces all that there is, means that our reality comes to be defined as essentially meaningless and destined to return to that first miracle from which it came. Within the scientific structures, this is a logical position as there are laws stating that the sun will expire and life that came from nothing will eventually go back to nothing. Residents have come to believe this, and have defined their purpose solely based upon the scientific measurements made by our sensory organs within this small picture plane, missing a much larger picture of process that cannot be measured or quantified.

Science is like a fire within our cave environments, illuminating what is closest to it, making what is beyond it even darker. We try harder to make the fire bigger and brighter, but only succeed at conditioning our eyes to the warm light, and not to the cold darkness that lies beyond. In this state, reality comes to be seen as what is closest and most measurable to us. We accept this on faith that it is our sole and complete reality. If a larger reality exists, then it must be described through the smaller reality, using its terms and logic, which essentially ensures that a larger reality will never be discovered. When a larger reality is expected to be contained within and derived from the smaller reality, our belief in this will inevitably limit our explorations to what is closest to us.

Through our desire for certainty, we have allowed our awareness to be trapped within these cave environments, ever remaining fixated on the artificial illuminations that are provided for us, and ever ignoring or attacking any phenomena that cannot be explained within this environment. Breaking free from these chains means becoming aware of our inherent limitations, recognizing that what the tools of science discover, do not, and cannot, throw into doubt that which they are unable to discover. It is to recognize that its successes within its limited environment do not cast doubt on those realms where its tools cannot function. Existing within the realm of certainty means not exploring and investigating all possible realms and states with humility, reverence and awe. Rather, it is existing in a state that is afraid of certainty coming to an end.

Religious structures also have many nested stories. Most often these stories are a reaction to living within Moloch's environments. These structures teach its residents that we came into this world with a corrupted human nature that is primarily evil, fallen and selfish. This belief naturally requires the need for Moloch's primary value of control. Under Moloch thinking, human nature must be put under control by the use of external laws and authorities – there must be kings. When we have succeeded in dominating our evil nature through various rituals and requirements, we then have our certainty. Certainty means that we have successfully controlled the outcome: heaven. Having grown up within the spheres of Moloch, the story of an evil human nature is not a difficult story to buy into. It is, indeed, the product of living in the environments of Moloch.

Through the structures of religion, Moloch has silently co-opted our desire for something more and used it to further extend its own reach. Stories create and guide action. Because of religion, new worlds are continually being colonized. Ancient wisdom and cultural traditions are being hemmed in and more people groups are submitting to this religious paradigm of control. This paradigm ultimately brings with it a view of the profaneness of matter. God and heaven are somewhere out there, and regardless of how we treat this world, we will someday be caught up into a rapturous escape from this prison. When our stories enforce a belief in the profaneness of matter and when matter is no longer viewed as sacred, it will naturally create actions that are compatible with Moloch's campaign of exploitation and destruction.

Another consequence of avoiding the pain of uncertainty with the divine is that the divine becomes merely a projection of the familiar. Humanity's understanding of God appears to have been, to a large extent, a reflection of their descent into Moloch, mirroring their environments and experiences. Man's view of God moved from early conceptions, where God was seen as becoming within every part and whole of nature, to a perception of a separated God that was removed out of nature, following man's own descent out of nature.

This new conception became a supernatural God, an elevated part that was separate from the earthly and natural realm. Through this gradual evolution, God came to be imbued with Moloch's qualities, being egotistical, jealous, angry, violent, controlling and demanding, requiring propitiation, sacrifices and offerings to appease his wrath. Our belief in our evil nature created these requirements and essentially created a God in the image of man. This appears to be a consequence of God, being described by man, a reflection of what man sees in his cave-like environments.

The consequences of this story do not stop with our view of God, but have slowly worked themselves into our view of nature. In many of the structures of certainty, there is an ongoing battle between good and evil. This belief has been projected onto everything. Wheat is good, but weeds are evil. Bees are good, but aphids are evil. Chickens are good, but foxes are evil. Grass is good, but dandelions are evil. Lady bugs are good, but mosquitoes are evil. This extends into every realm. Evil must be overcome. Nature must be overcome. And so, Moloch, having subtly co-opted humanities conception of God, gladly accepted their offerings in order to overcome evil.

Because we have cut ourselves off from a story that comes from within, we now require prophets, messiahs, scriptures, priests, pastors, laws, doctrines, canons and creeds – authorities and indisputable sources of truth outside of ourselves. The kingdom of God is no longer found within but has been transported to heaven. Under Moloch thinking, the only way to find this kingdom is through the structures of religion, as they hold the keys to liberation.

Having lost contact with our inner narrative, we have submitted to a craft of control that enslaves ourselves to static conformism. As the fortress of canons and creeds, statements of faith, confirmation classes and worship songs are built around us, group-think wins and free thought succumbs. We naturally assimilate and accept our psychological locks as the system is powerful, offering social rewards for strong members of this group-think and social punishment for weak members. We blindly accept what we are told, grateful for the self-important rewards of leadership positions and affirmations by the community. What is the need to grope about the darkness when certainty can turn us into mere consumers, receivers of a truth that is all laid out in black and white – and sometimes red?

Within the cathedrals of certainty there exists a pathological fear of the dark – of what cannot be brought under control to be directly examined. Through fear of the unknown, residents cling to illusions of certainty, remaining chained to their axiomatic systems, keeping them at a safe distance from any reality that may challenge the known.

There is truth in the promise of salvation within these structures. It is not salvation for residents; rather, it is salvation for these structures, which like all structures of Moloch, depend on the active cooperation and participation of each resident. There will always be realms of truth that exist beyond our limiting frameworks. If we wish to experience, touch and taste these fruits, we must first experience a liberation that can only come with the crumbling of certainty.

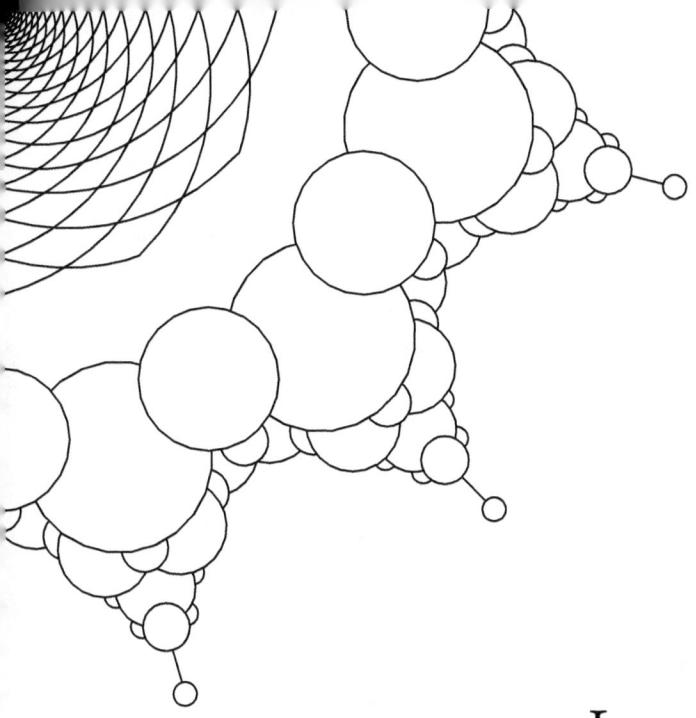

Lesson 377

Moloch in Their Eyes

Mass man wakes from an uncomfortable sleep, still tired from a mind that refuses to be still, constantly moving, assessing, worrying and planning. The environments he lives in create an enormous amount of stress, providing him with more to do and less time to do it. His senses are overloaded at the thought that he should always be doing something.

Upon waking, the first action of mass man is to reconnect with Moloch, plugging into its system through the constant ritual of checking the clock. Man's body is no longer timed to nature, the circadian day and its seasonal cycles; rather, it is forced to keep pace with time, another abstraction of measurement. Conditioned by Moloch thinking, his life submits to the guiding principle of the mechanical, daily consuming its products of seconds, minutes and hours. Whatever man does and whatever he receives throughout his day is done at an accelerated tempo, as he and those around him suffer from time scarcity. Pausing, or waiting, will cause him impatience. Doing nothing will bring about waves of intense boredom and irritability. His life is ruled by the clock. He only knows how to react, as there is no time to reflect.

Man's second act, upon awakening, is to connect himself to noise. Connecting to noise is his routine. Without it he feels lost, disconnected and uninformed. There exists within him an urge to be updated on what is happening in the world. He needs his dose of unseen propaganda and entertainment. He enjoys it so much that he conditions his children to it, turning on the noise for them too. Unknowingly, he is creating an environment where desire, centered on self, will rule – desire for products and images, styles and looks, food and gadgets, entertainment and stimulation.

What man has allowed to enter his environment is an impoverished reality that serves to further entrench his family into a system that separates them from touching or embracing what is real. What he and his family knows, sees, hears, tastes and feels is mediated for them by the products and creations of other residents of Moloch.

As mass man gets ready for the day, he starts with the mirror. The mirror has such a drawing and solidifying effect that he is almost incapable of passing by any mirror without looking at himself. The mirror, at times, boosts his ego, but it also creates more desire centered on this ego. His attention is drawn to those features that do not conform to the image of what a mass man should look like – an image that he has absorbed and incorporated throughout his entire life.

He seeks to replicate this image in all areas of his life. He picks out the most expensive, and the most visibly branded clothing and shoes. It is difficult, with his distracted mind, to think about where these articles of clothing came from or the type of slavery it took to make them. But even if these thoughts cross his mind, it is of no use, because his watch, the symbol of his own slavery, tells him that he has got to keep moving. He slips it around his wrist, believing it to be merely another adornment. He is prevented from seeing that his actions are a display of the bond he has with his master. To him, time is money. And he is obligated to keep a constant eye on where his master is going.

In his rush, mass man takes no thought to the food that he puts into his body. He feels no compulsion to question the taste, texture, makeup or origin of his food. He has been separated from real food for the duration of his life, only having access to food that comes from mechanical plants and factory farms, as opposed to food that comes from freeborn plants. His food fills, because it is filled with modified ingredients, artificial chemicals and preservatives, loaded with fats, salts and sugars. He is unable to notice these things as the ingredients are hidden behind complex words. However, he clearly sees the appealing boxes and claims, enticing him to consume these products in order to lower his cholesterol and lose weight. He pours milk over his food and puts cheese on his bread; yet, he is unable to see the destructive processes that produce more milk through better efficiency. Not having time to think, mass man quickly finishes eating his meal that has been trucked in from faraway places, and throws away its plastic wrappings, knowing that these, too, will disappear to some other faraway place.

Still pressed for time, mass man quickly gives his children their daily medication that their school mental health professionals suggested and their doctor prescribed. He does not see how his own children are a desirable market for drug manufacturers and their extensions, being compliant, lifelong customers for these industrial enterprises. Not only does Moloch create an environment that causes disorders, it actively seeks to find and diagnose new disorders in new patients. Under Moloch thinking, this is good marketing as there is unlimited potential for growth in this area. Even the psychological experts cannot see this, being so deeply invested and entrenched in the society of Moloch, they are unable to call into question where the problem might lie. Mass man is unable to comprehend all of this, only seeing symptoms through the labeling of the experts: hyperactivity, depression, mood disorders, oppositional disorders, sleep disorders, developmental and personality disorders.

Like the experts, mass man is so deeply entrenched in Moloch thinking that he does not learn and does not think to ask if something might actually be wrong with the systems surrounding his family. Instead, his thoughts and questions are directed towards control, asking himself how he can best control the symptoms through the new and various behavioral technologies. Through his actions, he unknowingly affirms to his children that the system is not the problem. Instead, it is simply the unfortunate luck of dealing with a random human disorder that could affect anyone at any time for unknown reasons.

Since his spouse has already left for work, mass man gathers the kids and gets them into his personal transportation vehicle, one he was seduced into buying through his screen. He believed the propaganda about luxury, style and progress, speed, efficiency and power, comfort, affordability and freedom of movement. He believed in it so much that he went into debt to buy not just one, but two – one for himself and one for his wife. He clearly sees what possessing this vehicle gives him but is blind to what it takes away.

Mass man fails to see how the automobile pollutes his air, soil, water and culture. He does not see how it propels the expansion, widening and repairing of its system of roads, paving over forests, fields and water, destroying the natural beauty of landscapes so that these vehicles can go to the places they want to go. Man does not see the increased need for metal and plastics. He does not think about where the energy comes from that propels his vehicle. He is not aware of the cost to extract, refine and transport, as well as the wars and deaths in order to control. He is blind to the life of those who have had to submit to routine labor for the majority of their life in order to produce these vehicles. He does not see how his vehicle facilitates the explosion of real estate and businesses in every direction, requiring the consumption of more and more resources. Mass man does not understand how this invention propelled farming into an industrial process and how its assembly line spread to all industries, resulting in a wave of cheap consumer goods. He does not see how the entire world is remade in order to accommodate the demands of this one technology, creating environments that essentially requires its ever increasing use if a person simply wishes to live. As mass man leaves his home, he is greeted by a congested commute and the desire for a couple more lanes.

In the back of his vehicle sits his kids, who each stare into their own portable screens as he moves slowly through the congestion in order to drop them off at their approved learning facilities. Whether he drops them off at daycare, preschool, public school or summer camp, it does not matter, as long as they are taken care of so that he and his wife can both be freed up to work. He feels distant with his kids but cannot understand why. But, with no time to think about it and no time for silence, a force compels him to turn on his own personal noise.

As he kisses his children goodbye, and tells them he loves them, he turns the noise back up and drives quickly from the suburbs to the city. He passes by the towering structures and marvels at their size, yet, he is unable to see Moloch where it is most evident. He does not realize that his city is a symbol of power and independence from the whole, a place of pure Technique where Moloch has successfully concealed life's metaphysical background.

Starved of contact with the natural world, mass man does not look up anymore. Even if he did, Moloch has already taken care of it by covering the sky with its own artificial light pollution. As man drives in his encapsulated vehicle, he does not realize that his vehicle, his city and even his shoes have encapsulated him from nature. Not only is the air in his environment conditioned, so too, is his view. What he sees is limited to steel, concrete and glass. He has no sense of contact with living environments as he is always surrounded by dead environments. His only acquaintance is with the machine and what the machine makes. He rarely touches anything that has not been developed, planned or engineered by a human being. He mostly sees art and architecture through the well placed veneers that hide the ugliness of what lies underneath. Even the isolated trees he passes by have been specifically placed in their location. So deeply conditioned to his environment, mass man only feels admiration for the power, creativity and ingenuity of man, further strengthening his ongoing story.

During his commute to work, mass man cannot avoid passing by the walking wounded. And yet, he is prevented from seeing how it is Moloch that wounds, then offers healing, all the while expanding its story of control into new domains. Moloch creates the demand for police, courts, jails, therapy, residential facilities and law offices, creating hurt people who only know how to hurt people. The trauma that Moloch thinking produces, ensures that the demand for these services will only increase, which further ensures that these services will continue to expand, causing even more of the problems that they are supposedly there to fix. It is these institutions that diagnose and respond to the symptoms of Moloch, and yet they are unable to see the cause – completely overlooking this hidden pathogen of the mind. Moloch in the mind, has spread itself to such an extent that those who are no longer infected by this way of thinking are now the ones who are considered mentally ill.

Mass man checks the time and quickens his pace since he must be punctual at his place of employment. In not possessing true freedom, he appears when beckoned, the onus of a slave to his masters. As he sits himself down into his cubicled cage, his only real protest is that he is not a big enough cog in this machinery. He sees how he would do things better through increased efficiency, all the while contributing to the frenzy of more bureaucracy, more departments, more executives, more rules, more computers, more paperwork, more procedures, more technicians and more depersonalization. Though he cannot see it, all around him are the monuments to this bureaucratic phenomenon: towers full of offices.

He dislikes his boss who appears outgoing, friendly, talkative and charming, but who is really competitive, aggressive, manipulative and insincere. He does not see how these are the reshaping of a personality to fit into an environment that requires it. Yet, even he copies this behavior when working with co-workers as he desires to move up the corporate ladder at all costs. He doesn't like his occupation; however, since the only real occupation is to make money, he is where he belongs.

There are times when thoughts begin to creep in that there must be more to all of this. He feels made to explore, discover and create – but the phone will always ring and he is quickly brought back to his mundane work where he sits at a desk with minimal motion for hours – hours that only seem to increase. Conditioned as a mostly unquestioning servant to his particular system, he cannot ask why he works the hours he does, why he spends more time in the office than with his family, why he must work for what does not really fill and why he is in this repeating image of itself that he cannot find his way out of.

Moloch, for its part, does not forbid the questioning thoughts of this mass man; rather, it guides these thoughts to the repetition of its own image. Naturally, his thoughts of 'why' turn into thoughts of escape – thoughts about how he might recharge his batteries so he can be more productive when he returns. This escapism is redirected into objects that will benefit Moloch's own profit and expansion, limiting his diversions within a spectrum of this repetitive image. Mass man longs for the weekend, a break, hours of screen time and sports. He looks forward to spending time with family and friends in acts of mutual consumption, whether it is church, seminars, restaurants, bars, sporting events, vacations, the viewing of confined animals or even camping in a designated nature zoo.

Freedom is only seen through the repeating image of leisure. It is even given a formal status within this realm called the weekend and vacation time. This time, though, is not free, as it had to be worked for in order to be earned. In his longing to escape his reality, man does not see how his own actions continue to create this reality. But, he presses on, knowing the hours he works provides him with money, food, shelter, possessions and insurance – safety and security. Unknowingly, he has allowed his time to be devalued and made into an object of commerce. His moments are sold for a wage and his time reduced to money. This medicine is cheap and effective, dulling the pain of his empty life. Moloch has become so deeply planted within his mind that he does not require coercion, as he has been conditioned since birth to accept his servitude.

When mass man leaves his job, he feels a sense of satisfaction for having finished his stint for the day. But, since his work has been fruitless – doing so much while doing so little – he feels the need to move his physical body. Life is essentially an immobile one and he must exercise in order to appear healthy and to try and maintain the look and shape of a mass man. He repeats the image of his life, doing so much while doing so little. He runs but does not go anywhere. He exerts force but has not lifted anything. Man accomplishes these movements within an environment of his liking: screens everywhere, noise everywhere and lots of familiar strangers to assure him that he is participating in something that should be participated in.

Mass man thinks he loves his spouse, but somehow, he also loves other women. What is most important in his life is fulfilling his own desires. When he arrives home he gives his spouse a quick kiss, but neither have much time for the other as both of their children need to be dropped off at an organized competitive sporting event. His children participate in very few activities that are not highly organized by experts. Coaches guide and teach his children in the art of competition and instill the value of winning within them. As a father he is reduced to a spectator and a chauffeur, living vicariously through his children's performances. But, even from the sidelines, he encourages his children in the values of Moloch. He cheers and he chides them, showing his children that competition is a serious activity and not to be taken lightly. He daily reinforces in his children's mind that they must be subordinate to the directives of their superiors, the experts and the coaches. He does not see how Moloch thinking has taken away his children's spirit of spontaneity, creativity and play.

As he pulls up to his housing development called Forest Ridge, where there is no ridge and there are no forests, mass man is reminded of his yard. He must keep a constant regimen of control to maintain his well-manicured lawn, a monoculture of chemically grown grass and occasional trademarked landscaping plants. He feels compelled to emulate a perception of luxury and sprays harsh toxins on what he perceives to be invasive species. These chemicals are so harsh that even his children must keep off his lawn. He sprays, mows, edges, weeds, fertilizes and waters, all so that his yard looks like a symbol of luxury and prosperity for those who pass by and also for his neighbors. His neighbors, who live within an arm's length of his house, are strangers to his family, devoid of intimacy, save the few exchanges of mutual greetings.

Moloch thinking does not end in his yard as he carries this thinking with him into his home. His home is a standard product of Moloch thinking, built without craft, without creativity and without affection. It looks exactly like every other house, built by residents who are not going to live there. It is a home for the mass market. It is a home for the mass man.

Much like his yard, the inside of his home is a place of constant control, where the processes of nature are kept out. Dust and decay are removed. The air is purified. Undomesticated life forms, such as spiders, ants and flies are eradicated. And the climate must always maintain a constant temperature, regardless of the outside environment. Though he does not understand why, his children have migrated indoors, feeling uneasy being outside in the not-quite-so domesticated realm. He does not understand why his family is suffering from allergies and allergic reactions to minor things like insect bites and pollen. He only knows control. Without thought, he goes and buys an extra air purifier and sprays more chemicals around the house to eliminate insects. He administers daily doses of antihistamines to his family in the hope of reducing their many symptoms. His family is unintentionally becoming more and more dependent on the system in order to solve the problems that the system is creating.

As the sun sets, his family is fed through the time saving device of the microwave and pre-made, prepackaged meals. The packaged meals conceal behind well crafted images the exploitation and suffering of the land and animals that it contains. The torture and violence of factory farming is hidden from his view, as meat does not come from the muscles of animals who want to live, but from grocery store shelves.

He tries to spend time with his children, usually through the mutual consumption of entertainment, but cannot see how his presence does not mean he is present. His awareness is captured by other things. Unforeseen to him, his children will one day move far away from his home, and he, like his parents, will be regarded as annoyances in old age, sent to a facility to be a problem for someone else. His death will take place in a streamlined modern medical facility, hidden from society and surrounded by machines, monitors and beeps. If he is lucky, perhaps he will find someone who will not let him die alone. Upon death, he will repeat the image of Moloch as his final act, encapsulating himself from nature in his very own luxurious coffin.

Before he retires to his bed, mass man is reminded of his need to take his evening medications, as he is suffering from autoimmune deficiencies. He has been conditioned, his whole life, to view nature as an 'other' – an adversary that is not an inseparable part of himself. The result is that his own body is rejecting itself, confusing some of its many parts and rejecting them as being a perceived adversary. He does not see how his actions towards nature inescapably create similar action towards himself. When his medication seems to be declining in its effectiveness, he only knows more. He seeks out newer and better medication, believing that someday he will find the right cocktail to fix his growing problems. The cycle continues, creating new problems that require more medication. Helpless against this vicious cycle, due to his belief in 'other,' he knows only control through conquest.

As the day comes to a close, mass man does not see that his actions and thoughts are typical of creatures who have been removed from their natural habitat and placed in an artificial environment. Like a creature held captive, he becomes dependent for his survival on whatever controls his reality. Naturally, he uses his brain to learn whatever is necessary to survive in this new environment. He conforms to the dominant patterns, spending his entire lifetime talking about stocks and sports, golf scores and politics – ministrations of Moloch. His environment has kept him under a continuous barrage of intense stimuli that he has simply come to accept it. His life has become habituated to Moloch's pace. Withdrawing from such an intense dose of stimuli would be suffering. Therefore, he condemns himself to maintain it, believing himself to be an adjusted and flexible person, accepting his reality as it appears to his senses.

At the end of the day, as he lays his head on his dust mite free plastic pillow, mass man has but a second to ponder a feeling that is bothering him. For within the depths of his soul, he finds himself to be a profoundly lonely man. Regardless of how big the crowds around him or how much noise surrounds him, there is, within, a deep longing for something more, something that he is separated from. To be lonely when surrounded by so much is to suffer. Knowing no way out, his thoughts simply coalesce around the need for more medication or an evaluation by a psychological expert. The pondering ends quickly, as the screen has come alive – it's time for the next episode.

Moloch has infected the mind of man to such an extent that he has been transformed into a metastasizing tumor – a cancer that has lost sight of its proper function. His actions have produced an imbalanced state that consumes whatever it finds on its path, growing at the expense of everything around it. Mass man is a form of constant motion and noise, throwing out the old to be replaced with the new, acting without understanding and following habits without investigation.

Being a cancerous growth, man is not aware that his actions are destructive. This is his reality. He is simply trying to survive. He did not cut down the forests, destroy the oceans or dirty his air. Rather, he simply lived – mowing the lawn, grilling meat, driving the car, watching the screen, doing what was required of him at work and finding ways to relax from it all.

This is only one cursory look at a few spheres of mass man within one particular culture. It does not, and cannot, explain every possible iteration of this story. Residents of Moloch exist at all levels, in all classes and in almost every society. They are constantly moving, growing and evolving into the spheres of Moloch. They are Moloch.

The hope, at this point, is that you would be able to recognize Moloch's story in whatever form it tries to cloak itself in and that you would be able to put the right questions to it. The wrong question to ask is: Does Moloch work? Because, it does. The right question that must be continuously put to Moloch is: What kind of work is it doing?

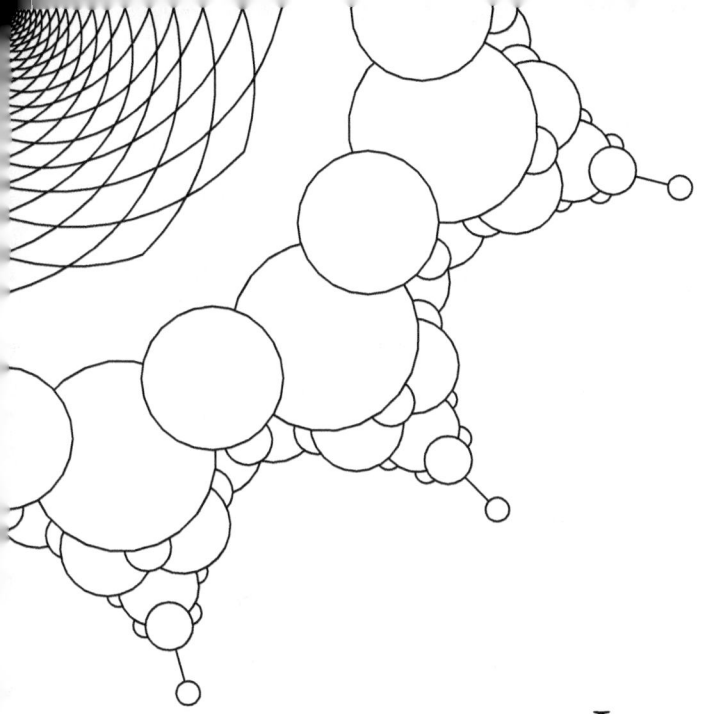

Lesson 610

Overcoming the Beast

When residents begin to glimpse the reality of Moloch, many become convinced that they can defeat this virus of the mind through external revolutions and reformations. History bears witness to the many economic, political, governmental, religious and agricultural revolutions that have been birthed throughout the ages. Nonetheless, with each new action, Moloch has evolved, developing new spheres and new structures where none previously existed.

Moloch is a powerful and crafty force. If we choose to fight this beast, we will lose. To overcome this beast we must not fight against it; rather, we must learn from it, understanding its purpose within a larger context. As we grow in our understanding, we will naturally start awakening to a perennial story that has always been written within. This story not only includes Moloch, but goes beyond Moloch.

The greatest source of nourishment for Moloch is to keep residents in an infantile state, as it knows, fully well, that energy will go where attention flows. Our world has, for the most part, become a reflection of Moloch thinking that loops endlessly throughout our minds. As participants of this story, our energies are put towards the service of furthering this story – we literally become the story.

If Moloch is to be overcome, we must turn our attention from its glowing spheres and throw ourselves into the terrifying darkness. It is only the inward path of selfless action that will guide us out of all of Moloch's spheres. When we start stepping down from the endless circles of Moloch thinking, only then will a larger story start to emerge.

This larger story, which has always existed within, can be likened to the latent energy that waits within a seed. When the conditions are right, the energy within a seed possesses enough intention that it starts to expand. As the seed expands, it can do no more than break open its seed coat, pulling itself through the dark soil that surrounds it. Eventually, the seed will break through to a larger story that may, at first, seem quite new. This story, though, is not new. It is not of a new age. It is an old story that has always existed – a continual symphony of those beautiful spirals that have been with us throughout all ages, extending into our deepest caves.

This symphony of spirals is always playing, waiting patiently for us to stop pushing and pounding random notes that keep what is beautiful lost within the noise. Noise will always keep us unbalanced, separated and distracted, making it difficult to hear what is beautiful due to the discord within our own life. But, it is this very separation from what is beautiful that creates the potential for awareness. Only in becoming aware of our unbalanced and inharmonious state, is reunion made possible.

Growing in awareness starts with throwing one's self into that uncertain darkness, bumping into what needs to be bumped into and finding the way out of all Moloch's constructs. Growing is a process. It takes time.

When you find yourself upon the boat of uncertainty, you must wait. Though it may seem like the journey is long, with no direction, and with no teacher, simply wait. There are other parts of you still trapped within Moloch thinking that are still feeling the pull of the spirals. Be patient, knowing that when you are ready, those beautiful spirals, through their unknown mechanisms, will start to be seen more clearly, drawing you past the corridors of Moloch into a strange and undefinable land. Solid, yet not solid. Visible, but somehow transparent. This movement is the process of changing stories.

In time, you will become aware of a great web of interconnected and intersecting spiraled paths. These spokes give support to the wheel of life, with each spoke going in only two directions. This is where you must attend carefully. Many have entered these sacred spirals and traveled upon their great arches, only to have changed their direction at an intersecting spiral, unknowingly placing themselves deeper into the spheres of Moloch and within a new structure of their own design. Ascending to great heights creates the potential for a much deeper fall. Such is the power of Moloch.

If you persevere, you will eventually begin to experience the inner sphere. This inner sphere is also a cave-like environment, as it, too, is a story we tell ourselves. Yet, strangely, this environment becomes more transparent the more it is traveled within, as it not only illuminates its own environment, but it also provides greater perspective and clarity to the many spheres of Moloch that revolve around it. Just as water becomes increasingly clear as its source is approached, so too, will the spirals.

Lesson 987

Story of the Spirals

Most stories require a beginning. As difficult as it may be, imagine the unimaginable – a primordial force that is infinite and boundless potential. It is everything and it is nothing. It is zero and it is infinity. It does not have consciousness, but is consciousness. It does not have existence, but is existence. There are no limits to this potential as there is no up or down, left or right. It just is. Alone with the alone.

Infinite potential, by itself, has no meaning. It has no eyes to see itself with. There are no surfaces to reflect its image. There is no separate mind to contemplate its being. This can be likened to light caught in a vacuum. Even though light exists, in such a state it cannot be seen, as there is nothing to reflect it. There is no perception of light. The light is darkness, one and the same.

Existence has no meaning without reflection. For this reason, existence becomes reflection, one becomes two. Existence is reflection. It is creativity eternally becoming limits by creating limits, not as a separated creator, but as the unfolding of creation itself. In order for it to be, it must be becoming. Such an abstraction is not conceivable as a noun, but rather as a verb.

This action of unfolding creation is the actualization of infinite experiences. To be is to be perceived, and so experience is actualized through becoming limits – matter to reflect light – the unfolding of potential. This unfolding is not desire, nor is it the lack of something; rather, it is creativity – the only way anything can exist.

Naming this process places it outside of its stream of becoming. To noun it, is to dethrone it. However, for the sake of communication we must dethrone it momentarily, temporarily naming it the RIDL: symbolizing the Realization of an Increasing and Decreasing Luminance.

The RIDL is the ultimate reality, lying beyond the scope of all human conceptual systems, beyond all human speaking and understanding, beyond our limiting personifications of it and beyond our domesticating of it. It is an eternal metaphysical something, the source as all, holding everything together, being pure awe and mystery. The RIDL cannot be understood with human thinking. Which means, there is nothing to hold onto other than mystery and awe.

This is the reason why the RIDL is so often named. A name solidifies, and solid things are easy to hold onto. Yet, understand that the naming of it, the personifying of it and the describing of it are ultimately nothing more than human attempts to describe the indescribable, using symbols that point to this ultimate reality that we long to describe in our imperfect and limiting ways.

Though we may try, the RIDL, by its very nature, is incapable of being caught in any verbal formulation. Words recoil as feeble attempts to describe that which transcends any particular expression. For this reason, metaphor, because of its ambiguity, is the closest we come to pointing to what lies beyond the picture plane that, at present, we cannot penetrate.

It is a delusion to believe that we can describe and understand the RIDL. If we could describe and understand it, then it would be no greater than our human descriptions and understandings, being confined to what our respective languages could define. Here, we must attend carefully, as any statement about it is a limit applied to it, and there are no real limits to limitless.

At most, we can imagine. To imagine boundlessness is to imagine something beyond limits. In order for something to be limitless, there must first be an experiential understanding of limits, as well as an experiential understanding of transcending those limits. This is another word for growth. In order for unlimited growth to be actualized, limits must find their existence within the infinite.

This necessitates the making of space to fit the finite within the infinite.

Most cosmogenesis beginnings starts with an explosion. In this story, though, its eternal cycle folds in upon itself with an implosion – an act of contraction. This can be likened to the natural pause in a great symphony or a blank canvas waiting to be filled. It is not known the number of songs or canvases that infinite potential creates, but what can be felt, is that our existence is one of these creative expressions we find ourselves to be a part of.

Actualizing potential, experiencing limits and gaining perception all necessitate separation, the emptying of primordial being into manifestation. When being moves, it is becoming. Separation creates the potential for reflection, and only in awareness of this separation do we find the potential for reunion. For this reason, being will sacrifice itself into limited space so that it can forget about itself. Decreasing luminance. Only then can it awaken to itself. Increasing luminance. Through these cycles the RIDL is able to experience itself at a much higher level – becoming, actualizing and filling infinite potential through the continual interaction of its many parts.

In a similar way that a light bulb has only a small resemblance to the energy created in a star, being stepped down through many nodes, we, too, are part of a tremendous source of energy that has been stepped down and made into accessible forms that are capable of experience and growth. In order for the RIDL to interact with itself, it must be broken down into smaller units that are let loose to explore and interact with an infinite variety of potential states. Each of these units is like a divine spark of light that learns in a cosmic game of hide and seek – exploring, discovering, gaining awareness and awakening to the ever present light within.

These sparks of becoming are not just limited to the human, but are present in all of existence, in every state of matter and in all things that interact, grow and learn. They are all innumerable modes through which the RIDL sees itself. It is through the multitude of these interactions that the RIDL can experience what would otherwise be purely conceptual.

Breath is the nature of all reality. Ascending from the many to the one is only possible after a descent from the one to the many. Breathing out, the RIDL empties itself into all forms, splintering itself into a reality of separate things and taking upon itself the sins of the world. New awareness, new experiences, new modes of existence and new realities. Breathing in, the RIDL eventually draws the prodigal forms home into its being. Cycles of being and becoming.

The descent may seem painful, but it is necessary, as only separation can bring about reflection. Reflection in turns brings about awareness and the possibility of an ascent to reunite with what has been lost. To awaken from our burial grounds in the depths of matter, is to see that we are the process of unfoldment.

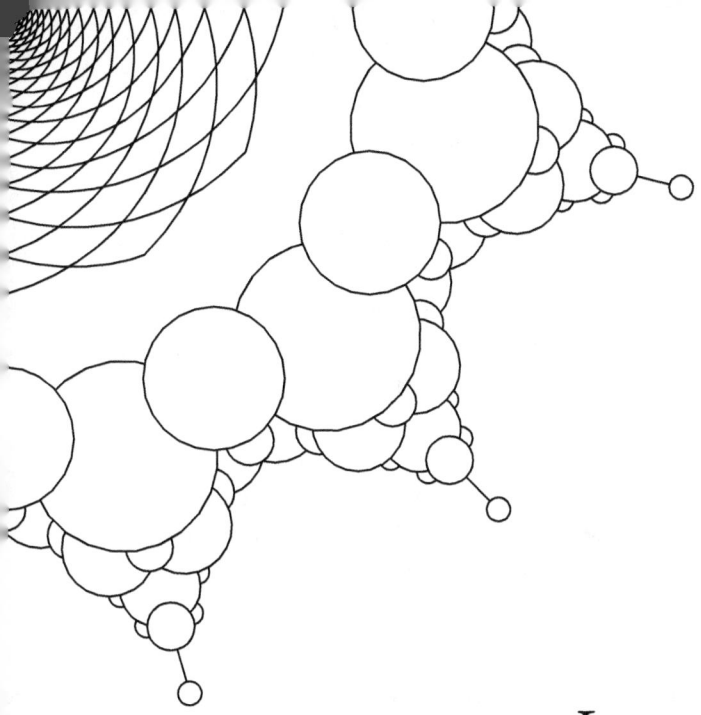

Lesson 1597

The Sacred Point

The unimaginable force of the RIDL emerges into dimensionality by a point of departure that penetrates the empty canvas. The point, non-dimensional as it is, is the process of introducing the RIDL into dimensionality and into limits. Just as the RIDL cannot be understood or conceived, neither can the point. They are one in the same, nothing and everything, zero and infinity, unmeasurable and unfathomable potential.

The point is the center of life's multiplicity. Everything proceeds from this point, being stepped down through division into many points. These many points are all of the same essence as the original point. They are simply arrangements of points, which are essentially creative arrangements of luminance. Just as a three dimensional cube is made up of two dimensional planes, and those planes are made up of one dimensional lines, and those lines are made up of mathematical points, so, too, does all matter, if traced backwards, condense into this undefinable abstraction – the one inferred by the properties of the many.

Without the many, the point is all one. It is alone. For this reason, the point can do no more than expand into possibilities, into perceived dualities, into this and not this.

The wordless language of sacred geometry helps remind us of this forgotten process. It shows how shapes relate to each other through harmonious recurring patterns, one in the play of the many. Through its lines, shapes and spirals, it represents, in visual form, the archetypes that hold up our reality.

Upon the blank canvas, the geometer creates a point with the needle of his compass. From here, he inflates the point to create a circle, separating the dimensionless space of nowhere into the infinity of points on the circle's circumference. The circle is a great mystery of incommensurability, as its circumference and radius are unmeasurable at the same time. To measure the radius in rational units is to find the infinite digits of pi in its circumference. To measure the circumference in rational units is to find the infinite digits of pi in its radius. One is the number of absolute unity. For this reason, the circle has become an important symbol that points to the mysterious nothing and everything of the RIDL.

The number one, whether found in a point or expanded into a circle, is still alone. The number one is only definable through the number two, the fracturing of unity. In order for something to be, to exist or to be perceived, it must acknowledge and negate its opposite. It must free itself from the repetition of its own image.

Envisioning this, the geometer moves to the furthest edge of the circle, reflecting the first circle by drawing another circle that intersects through the center of the first circle. This second circle demonstrates that all things take on existence through that which perceives them. Only through multiplicity is unity revealed.

Through multiplicity, the intelligence of things exists – the comprehending of states through the appearance of their opposites. Yet, in the number two, the number one still exists. Indeed, in all the divisions being made, the number one contains them all, remaining infinite, containing the thousands, millions, billions, trillions and beyond.

With two overlapping circles we now find the creation of a third space from which all other shapes and patterns are able to emerge: the vesica piscis. It is the inherent structure of this womb that contains the ratios of one of the most instructive and important patterns: the golden spiral.

The golden spiral is a beautiful, symbolic pattern that shows us how the uniting of different parts can blend into a deeper and richer whole. The structured unity within the golden spiral is really a multiplicity of parts that exist in balanced, harmonic and beautiful relationships. These relationships work and are beautiful.

Though the golden spiral is a great teacher, it cannot be understood by simply breaking it down into its numerical value. To do so is to insure that you will be lost within an infinite number of abstractions. This is one of the first lessons of this great spiral. It shows us, through its archetypal pattern, that numbers are ancillary, while proportion and relationship, are primary. Existence requires perception and perception is defined by the relationship to that which is being perceived.

Be still and observe this great teacher as she weaves through the grand tapestry of life. Observe her phenomenon of parts and wholes and how everything relates to everything, bound together and interconnected. Motion mysteriously condenses to create a whole atom. The whole atom, in turn, becomes a part of a greater whole called a molecule. This molecule becomes a part of a much larger new whole, the cell. The cell becomes a part of a new whole, the organism. Through a multitude of paths, this continues up and down through the spiral of life, creating bacteria, plants, animals, ecosystems, planets, solar systems, galaxies and the universe. It continues on until it comes back around again – a beautiful spiraling torus of being and becoming.

This is similar to how a movement of thought produces a written letter that is its own whole. This letter becomes a part in making a whole word. This word becomes a part in making a whole sentence. This sentence becomes a part in making a whole paragraph. This paragraph becomes a part in making up a whole story, and this story becomes a part in compelling the creation of new letters and new stories. At each level, parts work in harmony to create increasingly greater complexity. Regardless of the direction we are capable of perceiving, whether all the way up or all the way down, each whole is dependent upon its parts, and each part is dependent upon its whole, spiraling round and round with greater complexity and depth at each turn.

In observing wholes and their parts, we find each to have a function and a purpose that contributes to increasing wholeness, complexity and meaning. Each whole survives, prospers and grows through the contribution of its parts. A molecule will not function if its atoms are displaced. A cell will not work without the cooperation of its molecules. Organisms will not work without the help of cells. Likewise, a word will not work without its proper letters. A sentence will not work without its proper words. A story will not work without its proper paragraphs and chapters. Each part can only contribute to greater wholes by functioning as an interconnected whole where it is, maintaining its autonomy as a whole while simultaneously fitting in as an entangled part of its greater whole.

When parts and wholes do not cooperate in harmony and when they manifest disproportion and disharmony, a lesson is created. If lessons are not learned, disharmony will drop down various levels to be reused by some other movement that is seeking out harmony and balance. If the parts of a human body are out of balance for an extended period of time, they will no longer function properly and will decompose. The atoms will then be taken up into some other part/whole. Likewise, if a story no longer works or is unintelligible, it will eventually need to drop back down to letters to start the process again. And this is part of the process, expanding out into new and sometimes chaotic states.

Parts and wholes, in harmony, create a web of interdependence. Each strand of life is supported by other interconnected strands. Parts and wholes maintain their existence through playing with competition in order to discover cooperation. To diminish or impoverish any of these strands, to isolate a part, to consider it independent, is to introduce the lessons of disharmony.

This is the basis of Moloch thinking. When humans see themselves only in the light of their wholeness, believing that all parts revolve around them, and when they see themselves as the pinnacle of creation and evolution, forgetting that they are also a part in a much greater whole, their isolated and competitive view of life will inevitably produce a life of disharmony. And yet disharmony is a wonderful teacher.

Moloch teaches and reinforces the idea that life is about the survival of the fittest, control and competition. Naturally residents who hold to this belief see hunters and the hunted, winners and losers, invasive species, survival of the fittest, domination and the merciless tyranny of nature at every turn. But, when a much larger story begins to emerge out of our previous story, new perspective is gained and we are able to notice the opposite. We notice that nature is full of creative mercy, with a complex system of interconnected checks and balances that ensures a creative and growing whole.

Within this system, each part occupies its proper place, even if it means the sacrifice of a part. If the deer could be free from the tyranny of the wolf, the entire ecological system would suffer. The deer would multiply, eat and occupy beyond their proper place. The wolf certainly hunts deer, but it only hunts what harmony and balance have allowed it to hunt. When plants supposedly invade an ecosystem, they are trying to bring balance to what has been placed out of balance, covering soil that has been uncovered as if covering a wound so it won't get infected. This cover gives way in its proper time when balance has been restored. These organisms are not at war with each other. Their sole purpose is not to replicate and reproduce as quickly as possible. This is what a cancer does, a part that is out of balance with the whole.

Balance is the fulfillment and perfection of a part's proper place in the grand tapestry of life. To cooperate with the common purpose of balance and harmony for the whole is to succeed. To resist, is to ensure a life of competition and struggle.

Within our own bodies lies a beautiful system trying to maintain balance. There is a universe contained within our body that is not even part of our DNA. Within our bodies there are bacteria, viruses, fungi and a whole host of microorganisms that are, in the eyes of Moloch, not us. But, without these parts working together, we could not maintain an existence. For all beings, examples could be multiplied over and over again as life contains multitudes that cooperate and partner together in a dance that creates greater life. Cooperation is not just found in human or animal beings, but is ubiquitous, found in everything that moves. Life is all about exploring the chaos to discover new ways to cooperate. It is a collective, working through competition for greater wholeness all the way up and all the way down.

Everything in our reality can be seen as integral parts to larger wholes. Though the wholes may not be clearly seen or understood, this does not mean that the process of greater wholeness is halted. As human beings we are a whole – a vast collection of parts and wholes all functioning so that we may function. Each part in this great chain is equally important and an integral part of who we are, even if we are unaware of what that importance is. If the heart decides to no longer cooperate in the pumping of blood because it believes itself to be the center of everything, separate from everything and the last whole up the chain, then the entire system will suffer.

We, as humans, have done a similar thing. We have forgotten that we are part of something much larger and much more complex. In this great forgetting, we have placed ourselves at the center, experiencing ourselves as something separate from the rest, unknowingly throwing ourselves into Moloch's arms – a forced and chaotic state that is out of balance in its relationships to the community of life. This delusion of our creative awareness has created cave-like environments for us where our energy is focused on destroying the community of life that connects us.

This much larger whole that we are a part of may not be fully understood, but its design is captured and expressed within each part – the microcosm reflecting the macrocosm. Though we are wholes, we are not the end of the process; rather, we are one node of perception that is connected to all nodes. Within us contains a reflection of a much larger and more complex phenomenon. We reflect something higher in the same way that words point beyond their abstraction. The key is not to get trapped in the abstraction but to search out what these abstractions are pointing to.

Within all of us is the one. It is the foundation upon which we live, move and have our becoming. In every part, and in every whole, the one animates, fills and illuminates. The one draws and connects each part into a great spiral that, if noticed, will draw us back into a greater perception of the RIDL.

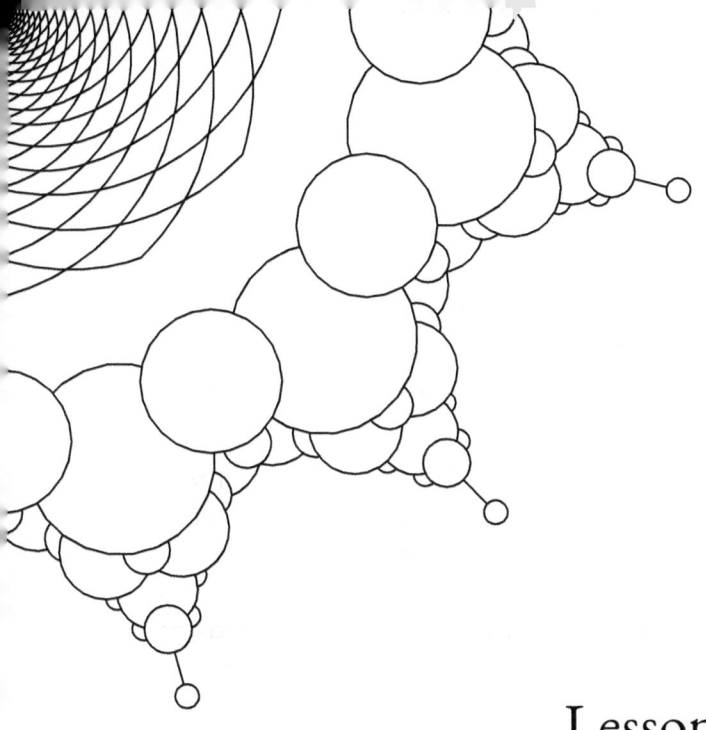

Lesson 2584

Learning Environments

The RIDL can be likened to a large fractaling pattern that is expanding its potential into whatever possibilities are available. Each node within this great fractal would appear as its own unique universe.

If we were to shrink ourselves to the realm of the atom, we would find a new experience of an enormous reality, equivalent to our universe, with auras of electromagnetic waves coming and going. Likewise, if we were to place ourselves within a cell, we would find a new perception of reality – a galaxy of movement with solar systems of interrelated transitory materials. The same thing occurs if we were to reduce ourselves to the size of a dust mite. We would, again, find another view of reality with strange looking creatures and environments, all exploring their unique states. These realities are as legitimate as ours and each has a higher purpose in their movements, even if it is not yet fully known.

Our fractaling node of reality, what is real to us, is like the layer of an onion. Each layer is connected and built upon the other. The particular layer we find ourselves in has its own walls that separate and provide boundaries between the layers of other realities. These walls are constraints of space and time that contain within them the very structure of the universe that our particular layer allows us to perceive. Our physical existence is one of many nodes of perception from which the RIDL is able to see itself.

All layers on this great fractal, with their unique set of experiences, are essentially learning environments. Every layer presents the RIDL with a perfect environment to explore and create new possible states. Within this system, individuated parts of the RIDL are constantly interacting, making decisions, remembering and creating. Because of this, each part has the opportunity to grow into something new. Each layer of this reality onion has the same mission and purpose – to grow into increasing harmony, balance, beauty, and unity. In all forms of awareness, growth is the key.

Our particular layer of reality is a learning environment. Moloch is a learning environment. We have a choice in this environment to either grow or diminish, ascend or descend, move towards the positive or move towards the negative. What often impedes our ascent is becoming overly fascinated with the particular cave we find ourselves in as our dense physical reality is a powerful enchanter.

Here-in lies the balance of existence. Though our layer of reality enslaves, it also liberates. Though it is an obstacle, it is also an instrument. Regardless of the life we find ourselves in, this reality is real and serves a valuable purpose. It possesses real meaning.

When we come to see our dense physical reality as a huge learning opportunity with a multitude of choices, decisions, states, paths and opportunities that drive the actualization of our part, we begin enacting the story that has always been written within. When we get trapped in the caves of Moloch and see our reality through the limited view it allows, we will inevitably enact its story.

Stories have consequences and direct our actions. To remain unconscious of these stories means that the lower things we find within our lives will not be seen as lessons trying to teach us of a different story; rather, they will be seen as the way things are – the only possible reality there is. To believe this is to create more opportunities for lessons to be learned. In this is a great hope, as the whole process lends itself towards patience, allowing discomfort and misery until it pushes our being towards greater awareness. Stories have consequences, so be wise.

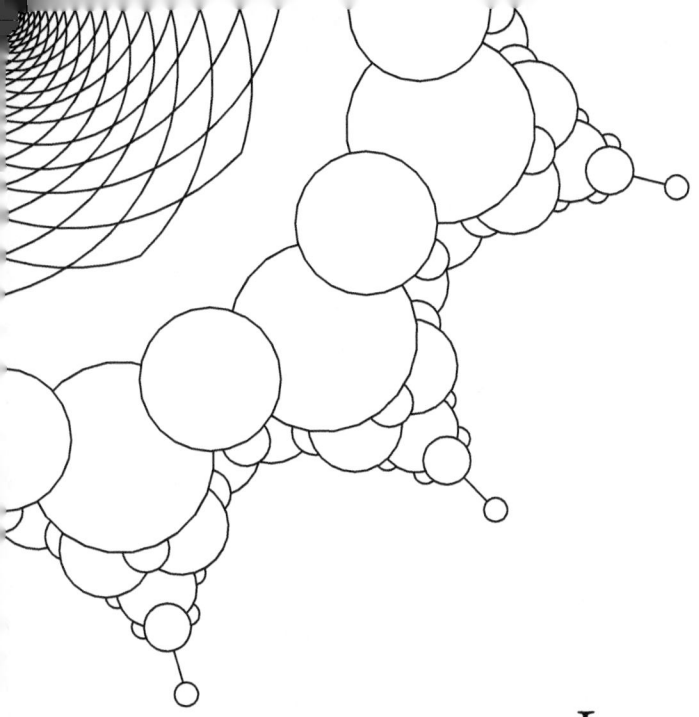

Lesson 4181

Necessary Evil

Reality requires polarity. Perception requires dualities. Experience requires opposites. It is in opposites, in dualities, that unity is freed from the repetition of its own image. It is free from the symphony of one instrument and one note. It is free from the infinite circumference of that one circle.

For there to be light, darkness must exist. For there to be one, there must be two. For there to be forgiveness, there must be offense. For there to be beauty, there must be ugliness. For there to be white, there must be black. White can only be seen because of its relationship with black. The existence of black makes white a possibility, as the existence of white makes black a possibility. Yet, there is no place where white begins and black ends as both are two ends of the same pole of color. As our perspective grows we come to see the opposite polarities for what they must be.

In order for potential to expand and create meaningful states and opportunities for growth and experience, there must exist the opportunity to mess up and to get things wrong. We could not know forgiveness without the experience of hate. We could not appreciate health and healing without sickness and pain. We could not know compassion and kindness in an environment that is devoid of evil and tragedy.

To look upon evil in this light is to understand that it has a rightful place – a necessary place. It is also to realize, that, if our learning environments were to do away with evil, then they would also have to do away with good. Light can only be recognized if it comes from darkness. Evil is a necessary condition for the realization of good. To see this duality and to comprehend it, means that the realm of darkness must exist and be experienced. Seeing darkness and comprehending it means that we are starting to understand the purpose of light.

The only way to see Moloch, is to live it, to be born into its structures, to experience it, and to find our way out of it. Moloch is a perfect learning environment that our own thinking created. It exists to reveal to us the imbalance and disharmony that exists within our part. We had to be born into Moloch so that the opposite of Moloch could be experienced and appreciated. Only in taking the wrong track, can the right one be revealed. It is the discord that brings us to an appreciation of harmony.

We have set Moloch up in such a way that it can lead us into hubris or into humility, into its labyrinth or out of it. Our separation within the depths of Moloch is not evil, rather it is our budding ground for self-discovery. It is the darkness that is the bringer of light.

Moloch is not an evil to be cursed, but a guardian to be respected. It is the embodiment of that necessary system of preparation and purification that will open the way to the spirals when the proper inner work has taken place. Without this necessary system, we could not form the capacity or the desire to understand harmony and balance.

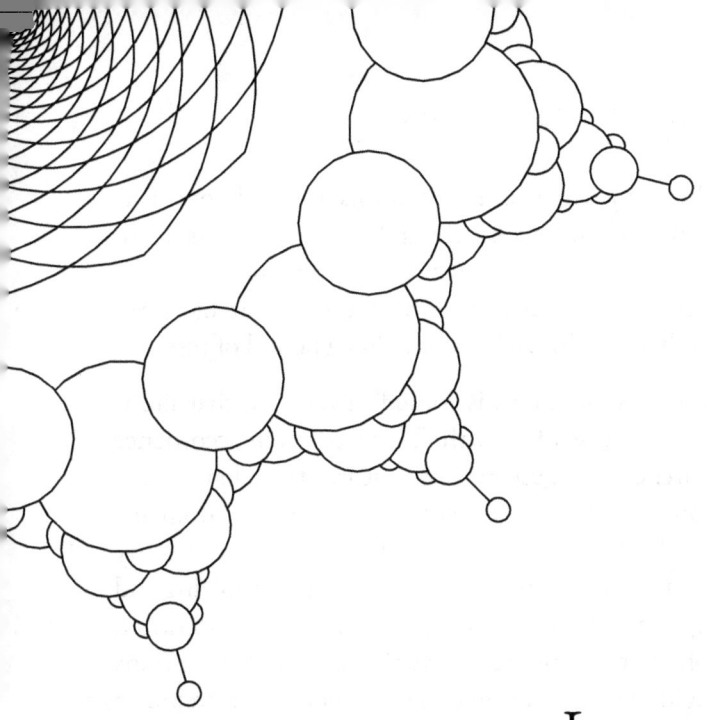

Lesson 6765

Cycle of Necessity

There is much to learn from the process that is often called a tree. Though its leaves are individuated units, they are all connected to a much larger and growing organism. The existence of a leaf is not limited to its own preservation. A leaf sees beyond its own individuality and its own span of life. Leaves are connected to the greater whole of the tree – a tree whose larger life necessitates the smaller life of the leaf. As the leaf grows and develops, it sends useful and vital energy to the larger life that gave birth to it. When the autumn winds begin to blow, the leaf does not fear death, but celebrates death with the throwing off of multiple colors as if it knows it is being drawn back into something larger. When its form finally separates from the tree, what once animated the leaf is no longer present within the form of the leaf. It has been drawn in, only to be drawn back out after a period of rest.

The story of spirals is rooted in the idea that life is similar to this process of growth. This story is in accordance with the archetypal gestures of nature that have been projected onto all planes of existence. Within all domains there exists a beautiful pattern of cyclical recurrence. Reality is filled with a multitude of rhythms and cycles, revolving and reoccurring patterns that daily try to capture our attention. These revolving patterns are not static, unaltered repetitions of cycles, rigid in space and time; rather, they are marvelously spiraled with every revolution being similar but never the same, moving up or down the spiral but never at the same level.

Our entire life is like a single day within a classroom of learning. Each day that we enter this classroom, we learn and grow in new and unique ways. Our grade level is chosen by the lessons that still need to be learned, the qualities within our being that have yet to be discovered and applied. The beauty of these learning environments is that each student is presented with as many opportunities as it takes for these lessons to be learned.

The same is true for those students who choose to ignore these opportunities. Many have fallen under the delusion that life has very little meaning. Believing in this story, they attempt to drop out of this learning environment by taking away their own life, only to find themselves back within a different learning environment and with new opportunities and lessons to aid in learning from their previous path.

Returning creates the potential for restoration. When the harmony within a spiral remains disturbed, it will return to that point of disharmony in order to seek out opportunities that compel its restoration. Any imbalance within our existence will eventually come around to teach us how to bring our part back into harmony with the whole.

We are a human instrument. To push and pound our keys is to produce dissonance that can either keep us in a distracted state, or aid us in discovering how to play our human instrument with harmony and balance. This is no easy task, taking much time and effort. In growing, we will inevitably make mistakes.

Mistakes should be embraced and not shunned. Through our mistakes, we are confronted with opportunities to ascend and learn by contemplating our errors and turning from them. This action nudges our part closer to harmony and balance. In this pattern lies great hope, because if we fail in this life to correct the deficiencies within our part, we will be given another. This process works much like a parent who actively educates their child. They work patiently with their child, giving them as many lessons as needed and repeating certain levels if the concepts are not grasped. As the child grows and his learning has quickened, levels can be more easily passed.

To better understand this process, imagine these learning environments to be like a great stage act. We don our costumes and our masks, and are given certain roles to play. Yet, these roles come without a script. Something hidden deep within us hides behind our many different masks. It is an anonymous presence, continually transforming itself in reaction to the role being played. Within this great drama, most of the roles we play are quite difficult, and yet, the choice is ours as to how we are going to create, improvise and actualize, regardless of the role we are assigned.

This dense drama that is unfolding before us is all the more difficult because we have been born onto this stage. Naturally, we have become fixated on our own mask and on the masks of others. Even though the presence of these masks and their props continually point to that which animates them, we become lost in our roles, worshiping the symbols, forms and appearances. In doing so, we forget the purpose of our role playing. Only in going inward and dissolving our preconceived ideas about these changing forms in which life is embodied, can we move up the layers to begin discovering the RIDL that ultimately animates everything.

Within each role we play, there is always the opportunity to follow the path of lower things, actualizing into reality that which causes disharmony. This is where the great stage act will provide us with new costumes, new masks and new roles to play. This is not so much a punishment as it is an opportunity to learn from experience. To have caused pain to another, it is then necessary that we, the perpetrators, would have to experience this pain for ourselves. If not, our experience would be incomplete and unbalanced, only understanding the side of the perpetrator and not of the victim. Once the experience is complete and growth occurs, it becomes difficult for us to actualize disharmony onto this great stage knowing intimately the pain it would cause.

The inequalities of human birth and the infinite number of ways we suffer are more than the blind mechanics of heredity or an unlucky lot in life chosen by a creator or by chance. Instead, they are most often the unseen law of compensation at work – cause and effect, action and reaction. Every temptation, pain, limitation, deformity and state, whether rich or poor, healthy or sick, contains an educational purpose. What we do to others, we do to ourselves. What we measure in others, is measured in us. In what we sow, it is eventually reaped within us. This unseen law is not about compensating some debt that we owe, but rather, it is about fixing a deficiency within our part. When our physical bodies have a deficiency or lack something, they cannot properly be healed until our bodies are supplied with what they are missing. Our deficiencies within our part work in similar ways in that they are deficiencies of higher qualities.

Ultimately, our learning environments serve a valuable purpose. They provide opportunities to grow the quality of our part and awaken the sleeper, making us aware of what we were previously unaware: our true identity. If we choose to remain unconscious and deny this identity, we will create the existence of future learning environments for ourselves so that we might have the opportunity to move beyond the spell that has held us. This law of compensation is not forever binding. In every environment, there exists that which fulfills the law of compensation and transcends its cyclical spell: the actualization of love.

Love does not reproach those who suffer as those who deserve it. Love does not assume to know the lessons that others are suffering. Love is not unloving. If we fail to show compassion upon the community of life and in the struggles of those who may possess lower qualities within their part, we will bring about the corresponding learning environments within our own life to help fix those deficiencies. Regardless of the layer and regardless of the situation, love amplifies the lessons of suffering. To be shown love and compassion when it is most needed, is to illuminate the beautiful spirals that we must all learn to walk upon. Do not assume that you know what lessons people need. Do not attempt to figure it out. Simply allow the process to be what it is and love in whatever way that is possible.

When life is seen through the eyes of the spirals, it is lived out from a different mode of being. Moloch's goals and priorities are no longer what life is about. Life becomes imbued with purpose and meaning, with every moment being an opportunity to prepare for the glories and infinite possibilities that lie beyond our current picture plane. It is a life of responsibility and a life that no longer projects its difficulties onto things outside of itself. It is a life that no longer needs the craft of kings for its own salvation. It is a life that fears no evil, holds no grudges and possesses no anger towards those who possess lower qualities within their part. These sleeping parts are immediately recognized as those who are simply on a different path of development, with many hard lessons still to learn. Though evil may temporarily reside in residents, it is not a quality that belongs to them.

In this light, sin is a state of disharmony – not being in harmony with the divine upward movement of life and making mistakes because one has yet to attain a higher level of awareness. It is action without perspective – selfishness due to short sightedness – an underdeveloped part. Nonetheless, an underdeveloped part is still in the process of developing and learning by creating an increasingly dense reality that will ultimately compel it to discover wisdom. What is most important when encountering these parts is to recognize it as an opportunity to actualize higher qualities like patience, forgiveness and compassion into reality.

In learning how to grow and peel away that which blocks the light, we inevitably become of great value to all those who we come into contact with. When perspective is gained, we are then able to live a life that shines even within the deepest caves. Going beyond limits, does not mean that those still trapped in limits are forgotten. When all layers are connected, all layers cooperate. This is why many have entered this grand experiment in order to help others grow beyond their previous limits.

Reaching the spirals and traveling back upon their arch takes time. There are no simple sayings of intent or any shortcuts to be given by those who peddle for money that which should be freely given. There are no professions of faith that will create an immediate change. Life is a process. Process must be experienced. Through this experience we will naturally experiment with different ways of becoming. This creates opportunities for learning – discovering through trial and error what works, what nourishes the soul and what is beautiful.

Even though learning can be a long and slow road, it is here upon this road that we find a great hope, as all things are working together for the good. All states, movements, moments and circumstances, regardless of how difficult they may seem in the present, are exactly what they need to be, when they need to be. There are no accidents. To truly understand this means living a life where there exists nothing that can hinder us; rather, everything is here to help us. It is a life no longer filled with problems but with opportunities to actualize higher qualities, to learn and go beyond what went before.

Being born multiple times may seem like a strange idea, but it is no stranger than being born at all. And yet the same you that entered this world is not the same you that will leave it. Your mind may appear to be limited within the box of your brain, but it is a deceptive box with a false bottom. It goes far deeper than this story could describe.

Ultimately, the story of the spirals is just that, a story. It points to something beyond itself. And yet to believe in such a story creates a new way of becoming. It means that there is no fear in life or death, for when this physical vehicle has served its purpose and death knocks on our door, it is not the end, but the return. It is the dying of the old and the birth of the new, growing and transforming into something greater than what came before.

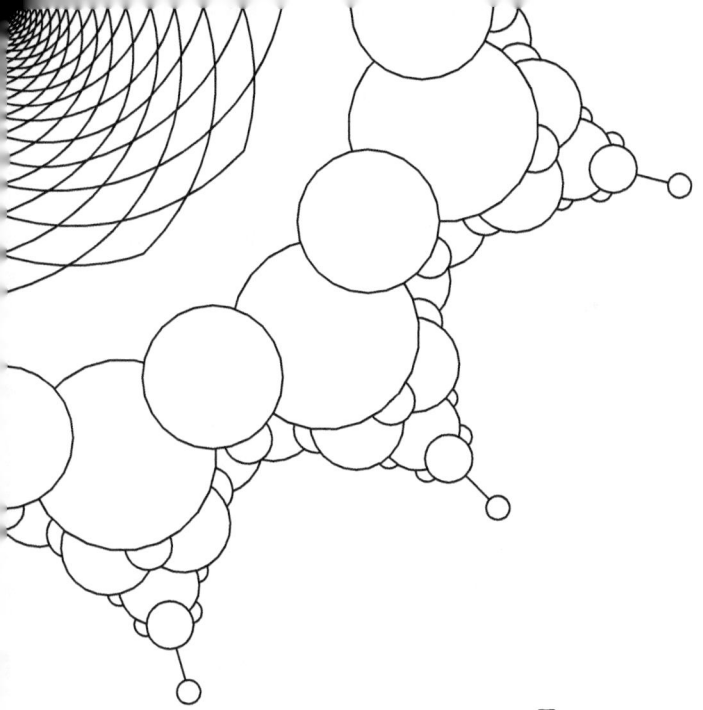

Lesson 10946

Purpose

Under Moloch thinking, our purpose is to survive. Under the story of the spirals, our purpose is to grow. The very act of perception creates change in the perceiver. To be, is to encounter becoming.

Belief in the story of the spirals is the recognition that we have placed our part into the alchemical fires of space and time for the purpose of purification and growth. It is recognizing that, in every encounter and in every situation, we are presented with opportunities to ascend or to descend, to stretch and grow or to constrict and withdrawal. It is to understand that with every birth into matter, we are presented with material environments that provides us with unique opportunities to transform the quality of our consciousness. It is to set ourselves upon the timeless journey, returning our movements to that which imagined it. Within the realm of Moloch there are only problems to be solved. Within the realm of the spirals, there are only opportunities to help us grow.

This is the same path of attainment seen throughout the ages. It is the perfecting of one's part in this earthly layer, preparing the soul for its journey through higher layers. To be seduced by physical matter and stuck in the illusion of self is to impede your growth by blocking the light within. This is done by adding selfish desire, control, pride and hate to your part – lower things of the descending path. When these things are peeled away and the blocks are removed, we get down to what is left: love, the purest form of movement. This is the ascending path – the path we all eventually must take.

Love cares for the parts, the wholes, and the whole. It sees everything as being imbued with purpose, an organic necessity that cooperates to explore, experience and transcend all available states. Every part is a sacrifice for the increasingly greater whole and each is its own gift of perception.

Perception is a gift we find ourselves holding. Gifts are not to be hoarded or hidden, isolated like the economics of Moloch and only used for the increase of pleasure, security and control. To waste this opportunity on the accumulation of things, on the learning of meaningless facts, on mundane and destructive work, on the descending movements, is to ensure ourselves of a dropping down and repeating, which, in turn, may provide some difficult learning opportunities.

An error can live many lives if it is not learned from. What man sows, he will surely reap. What he does to others, he does to himself. To hate is to draw hate to yourself. To be violent is to experience violence. To ridicule is to be ridiculed. To harm is to be harmed. To show no compassion is to find yourself impoverished. But, to love is to draw love to yourself. To be content is to draw contentment to yourself. To show compassion is to draw compassion to yourself.

Drawing yourself out and turning from the wall and its shadows means seeing the place where we now stand with new eyes and new clarity. It is experiencing the mystery in every movement, in every moment and in every state. It is seeing each life as being imbued with purpose, like a piece of a puzzle bringing the whole into greater realization.

Attend carefully. For many have set out upon this path, only to be unknowingly thrust back into Moloch's many structures. This quest is not a prize that can be won. It can never become a static victory. Instead, this prize is contained within a process. It is a journey that must be experienced, with each victory being one step in the process of greater becoming.

Every journey starts with a step. The first step, and the first act of conscious responsibility, is to become aware of our separation. It is the call for the sleeper to awaken to the stories surrounding him. We are co-creators in this process. By believing in the story of Moloch, we become unconscious creators and give it greater density. We make it more real and more powerful, giving it more of our vital energy.

When we begin understanding the purpose of Moloch, our movements will be done with more awareness. And yet, we will still exist in a world completely made over by Moloch. It must be this way, as alchemy cannot be performed without fire. Moloch is doing exactly what it needs to do. It is helping make that which shines. The spheres of Moloch create the most perfect environments for parts to learn balanced and harmonious ways of relating to the whole.

It is not our purpose to fight against Moloch or to destroy it; rather, it is our purpose to grow beyond it. When we move beyond the spheres of Moloch, we will see it for what it is – one step in the process of becoming, transforming our part into something greater.

When the light of every part is released from the grip of illusion, it can do no more than be drawn back to its source, like iron shavings being drawn to a magnet. This is a powerful movement, assisting and inspiring the repetition of this inward movement throughout all the spheres of Moloch. As this process continues and grows, Moloch will come to be deprived of its parasitic nature and will return to its source, reabsorbed into the point from which it came. And all that will be left of Moloch is our gratitude.

You are not a forsaken product of matter. There is real purpose in this time and place. However, do not think that your purpose is to transcend this dimension that your senses necessitate the perception of, to live on different planes, to leave behind these physical forms and get off the wheel of life. Someday this will take place, as this form will pass into another, but the question should always be, what will this form have added to the whole? What gifts have been brought back?

There is a reason we find ourselves within our particular reality. We all have areas in which we need to grow, lessons we need to learn, limitations that must be overcome, trials and tribulations, joys and passions that must be experienced, pain that must be felt. The process of life is the very purpose of life.

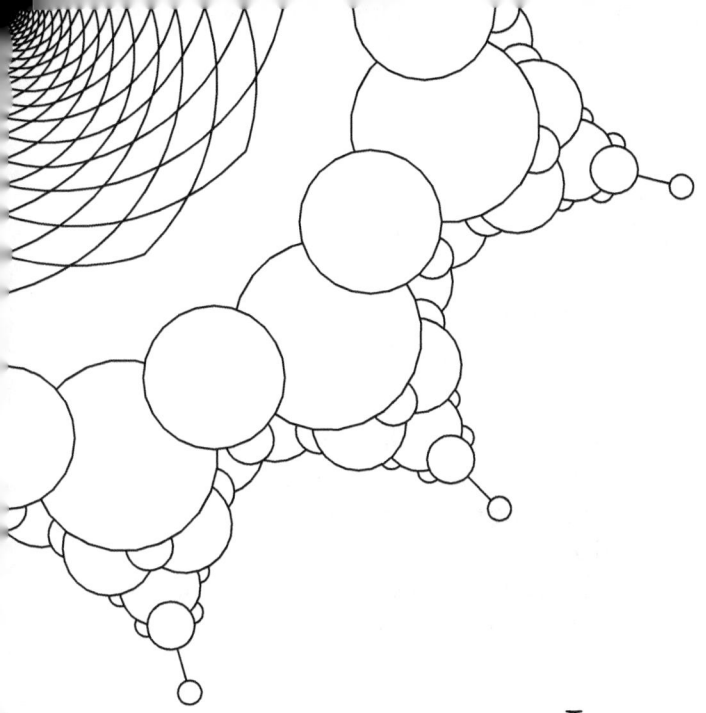

Lesson 17711

Experience

Our belief in limits defines the boundaries of our reality. Stories are real things, producing real action, and creating real environments. We unquestioningly believe in the story of Moloch and unknowingly propagate it because it dominates our total experience. The limits imposed on us by Moloch are the limits of our world. To go beyond limits is to venture out into the unknown, into the darkness. This is where growth happens.

Growing is not easy. It is extremely terrifying and quite painful. The story of the spirals is not something you can believe because you have read about it. It cannot be enacted by wishing it were real. To truly encounter the much larger picture, the spirals must be experienced. They must be felt.

Moloch is its own layer of this reality onion. Going beyond it means merging into a higher layers that encompass and include Moloch. During this movement to a higher level, as you hold onto that boat of uncertainty, you will start to gain perspective and greater awareness. With time, you will be able to see Moloch more clearly and more easily recognize its evolving spheres.

Moving inward means moving into something else, bumping into new things and experiencing new phenomena. As we move inward, we cannot help but continue to learn and grow. Limits are transcended and new realities open before us that show themselves to be somehow more real than any other reality experienced.

As spirals start to be seen, your spiritual eyes will start to witness things that would previously have been unthinkable. This is the opening up of your inner dimensions. And yet, these dimensions will forever remain a theory if they are not experienced. Spiritual transformation cannot be approached through mental concepts such as hearing about it and choosing to believe it or not. Rather, it requires your active participation to see this process with new eyes.

When we begin allowing ourselves to be drawn beyond the borders of Moloch, we will start to experience what lies beyond all verbal or written descriptions. These words will then be seen as crude and elementary at best. As we move into the spirals, all of our concepts will naturally come crashing down. It is here that we will inevitably realize that all of our words and all of our descriptions are just pointing stories that must eventually melt into what is.

Many of our spiritual ancestors have been molded and influenced by touching the realm of spirals, documenting their experiences in the language of their time. Many residents will remain content reading and wondering about these testimonies, yet fail to realize the same realm is right in front of them. Choices are always before us. We can grope among the dry bones of the past. We can read about those who have beheld the divine. We can hear stories and read poetry about great revelation, and we can choose to believe these or not. But, there are other choices. We have the option of seeking for ourselves and using our own perception to find what many who have gone before us have already found. This choice requires a pure heart as well as the courage and faith to let go. It does not seek power, fame or control.

Those willing to confront the darkness of uncertainty, will eventually discover the wisdom of the spirals. Some of these spirals may even provide a look beyond the shadow world of our human-centric layer by opening up glimpses of realities unlike anything ever experienced. Traveling to these inner worlds requires much wisdom because of the temptation to cling to the visions. To explain or circumscribe these experiences, will open up a path to be thrust back into the spheres of Moloch.

Take caution when higher realms are touched. We exist within our present reality for a reason. It has a purpose. Great care must be taken to ensure that our motivations do not arise from an unbalanced desire to escape our reality.

Instead, our motivations should come from a part that is responding to the inner call of growth. If we become obsessed with higher realms, we will ultimately forget the purpose of this realm.

There is a great danger in grasping for higher things. Higher things are not to be grasped at and may leave the crosser of this threshold with fantastical images that possess neither clarity nor cohesion. Do not despise your reality; rather, set yourself on a course of increasing clarity – seeing life's daily circumstances as opportunities for growth. Grow where you are planted and love what you are capable of loving. Use the glimpses of higher things as opportunities to gain perspective within your present reality. Recognize them as important teachers in the refining of your part, but do not be obsessed with them.

The RIDL is not within the process. It is the process. It is vital to trust the process. To forget that the process, is the purpose, is to create new opportunities for Moloch to build a sphere around you. Do not fly before you are fledged. There have been many who stumbled upon glimpses of higher things and suffered immensely, having been pushed further down the descending paths.

The knowledge of higher things is open to all, but it is the fool with his passions, being too quick with his feet, that misses the way. When you arrive at that boat, wait patiently. Let go of your expectations and do not try to paddle with your hands. Your boat will move when you are ready.

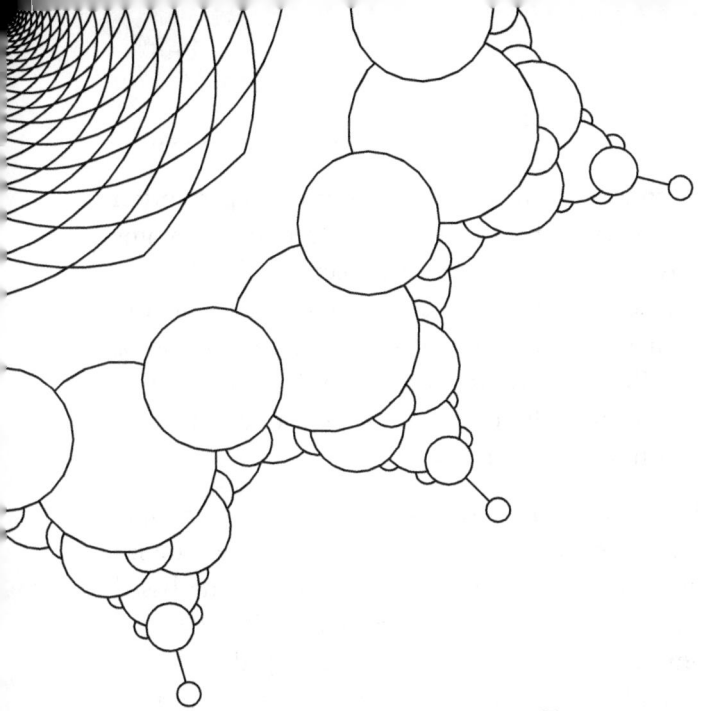

Lesson 28657

Humility

When you see, taste and touch, you will never be the same. As the story of the spirals becomes clearer, as you begin to experience more and more of it, and as you begin looking beyond its transparent walls to what the story is pointing to, one idea that will grow within is a deep realization that humility is the only way forward. Along the journey towards harmony and balance, what becomes evident is that only a small piece of a much larger veil has been lifted for us, opening ourselves up to the realization of how infinitesimally small our understanding really is.

Our understanding is similar to our visual perception within our current layer. Human perception contains limitations, as we only perceive a small section of an infinite energy band. Seeing with new eyes, beyond the physical, means expanding our vision to see a much larger portion of this spectrum. But, it is also the realization that there will be even newer eyes that will be needed in order to continue to see further. Each step in its proper time.

With increasing awareness comes increasing humility. When we walk upon this path, we find we are no longer as quick to reach conclusions and judgments based upon the narrow limits of our perception. This kind of humility cannot be willed or purposely developed; rather, it must emerge and grow as our perception of the larger picture emerges and grows.

To better understand, we can compare our limitations to those microscopic organisms that partner with us for greater health. Even though they play an important part in our development, they, like us, are most likely prevented from seeing and understanding the whole. They may observe things coming into their realm from beyond, but they would likely have a very limited understanding of what a human body is. The same limits could be imagined within the cells of our body. These cells work and function within a layer that their higher layers require. Yet, they likely possess very little knowledge of the greater whole they contribute to.

It appears to be the same for us. We may have some idea of the existence of higher things. We may understand that higher layers have their own functions, lessons and areas of growth. However, to assume that we can grasp a complete knowledge of these things, within our present layer, would be the same as believing newborns could grasp the thoughts and dealings of their parents. Though their parents love them and supply them with all of their needs, there is a great chasm of understanding between the two.

This is what it means to live in the mystery – to cooperate in its processes – yielding to the part and purpose we find ourselves in. The goal is not to search out a definitive answer or to believe in the illusion that we could even arrive at one. Rather, our goal is to live in and through the mystery – becoming in the process of greater becoming.

True humility is found in the darkness that calls us. It is found when we drop all of our inherited and preconceived notions of what is, so that 'what is' can start to tell us about itself. This is terrifying to Moloch thinking but absolutely liberating to our part. Here, there is no pride or arrogance – only humility, awe and wonder.

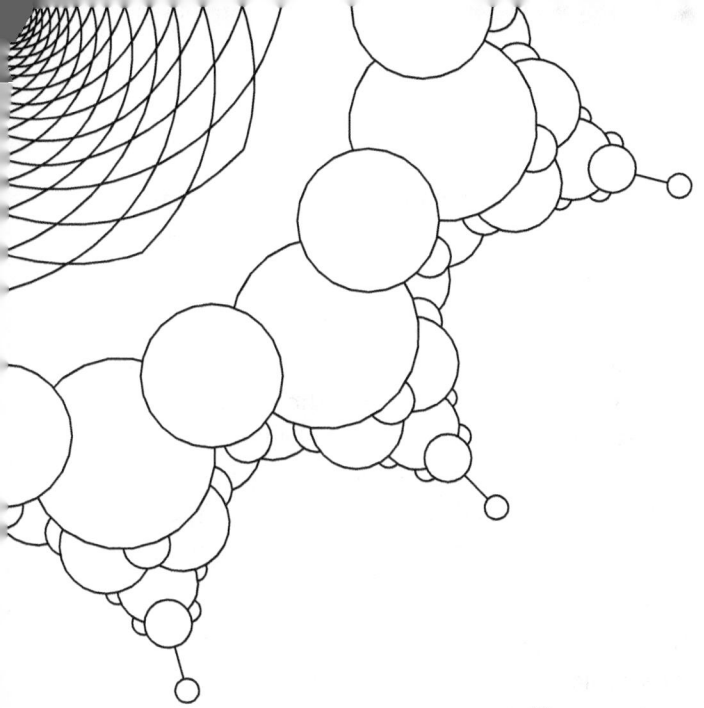

Lesson 46368

Truth

To possess this deep sense of humility is to see truth as being much larger than our layer specific scientific or religious truths. When we expand our perception and open up to a much larger picture, we will inevitably focus more on the purpose and relationship of parts.

Within the story of the spirals, truth is not a fixed state of things; rather, truth is a process. Truth is what is real, and what is real is that which is in the process of becoming. Truth is not only the underlying cause of all phenomena, but it is also the purpose of all phenomena. If this purpose is incoherent, then the underlying cause will be unbalanced. Truth will remain hidden.

Reason has its place and is helpful within its proper context, but when the illusion of certainty is seen through and the desire for control is surrendered, those small truths that reason has uncovered are then approached with greater perspective due to the much broader light of big truth – the RIDL. In seeing small truths through the light of big truth, we come to the realization that small truths have nothing to fear.

This freedom of perspective naturally compels us to examine, disassemble, and test whatever is said to be true without fear of its findings. This is especially important in dealing with what we already believe to be true. When that which is true and right becomes capable of withstanding our onslaught, we should be persuaded by it, and follow it. This is genuine skepticism, and it is an ally to big truth. It is not the enemy. Truth is not inconvenienced by such things. Though, if what is said to be true flinches or moves, we should adjust it. If it runs and hides, we should let go of it.

Even though such a pursuit of small truth is wise and will serve us well within our present reality, as we proceed out of the caves of Moloch it should become clear that truth is not always so black and white. Taking reason as far as it can go has its place and proper function within our reality, but there comes a point that reason can take us no further. With a larger perspective in view, our purpose ceases to be about gathering more and more information, lost in the labyrinth of the provability of truth. Rather, the larger perspective sees ourselves as creators and choosers of what is true and right.

With a higher perspective, the question is not so much about provability, but more about integrity. When we experience and interact with the phenomena of this world and truth claims are presented, the question from a higher perspective becomes whether this interpretation of the world is consistent with the reality that we choose to create. Does it contribute to a reality that we would choose to live in, and is it consistent with what we are becoming? In aligning what is true, right and good with the sacred spirals, we become co-creators of our reality. Truth becomes not so much about provability, but much more about whether or not it aligns with beauty. Is it beautiful?

What we believe to be true will give shape to our reality. We all have stories that we create and are created by. Stories, regardless of whether or not we are conscious of them, will ultimately determine our actions and our experiences. If our stories reflect harmony, balance and beauty in their relationship to every part and every whole, they will show themselves to be correct. Truth from the perspective of the spirals is discovered by the result of its application. If there are poor results from its application, then this idea of truth is irrelevant and useless.

Within our own being, if we are to see if there is correctness in understanding – if there is truth – we must look in the direction of our actions, at the stories we give life to and at the qualities growing within our part. The question from this view is not so much whether something is right or wrong, but whether or not that something is helping us improve the quality of our becoming? Is it leading to growth and to those higher qualities and attributes that are beautiful? To understand truth is not simply to have taken its measure;

rather, it is to come to understanding by way of relationships and experiences – an intimacy with that which is.

As you move inward, away from the spheres of Moloch, there will be truths that once served you well at an earlier stage, but inevitably, will become obsolete at later stages. This is a natural part of growth, as lower branches give way to higher ones. Real growth is married to humility, and here, there is no clinging to truth, as it is understood that the realm of truth is far greater than our present framework for understanding it. New knowledge only emerges from what we once thought we knew. What knowledge and perspective we may gain on our ascending path will make what we now know look rather simple and incomplete.

For this reason, we must learn to embrace our limitations, making every effort to write in pencil and not in pen – walking in others shoes and seeing our own blind spots by actively sitting in the seats of others. It is the illusion of having sufficient knowledge that keeps us from gaining new knowledge. Intellectual humility starts with recognizing that absolute certainty is impossible for limited parts. Absolute certainty requires the continual experience of every part and whole, all the way up and all the way down. To claim this certainty is blind hubris.

At best, our goal is to be open to provisional truths. These are not only answers that give the best explanation for things at the present time, but also answers that are beautiful. Truth exists; but, we must not be so arrogant to think that we know it. Truth, and our perception of that truth, may be two very different things. For this reason, avoid creating rigid mental maps and fight against the automatic rejection of any new idea, especially on areas you are least familiar with. The recipe for entrenchment in any system is to be satisfied with your knowledge and content with your own opinions.

As you begin moving into the realm of the spirals, you will find that it becomes much easier to embrace error within your becoming. Acknowledging error is not a sign of weakness; rather, it is a sign of refining humbleness – a sign that demonstrates growth. Those that are unable to accept error or the possibility of being in error, are wholly incapable of moving forward. They will continue to be apologists, passionately defending their own communal dogmas within the walls of Moloch.

This is the sphere of certainty, where pride assumes that we unequivocally hold the correct version of truth. The result of this is that we look no further. We become inflexible and automatically disregard contrary evidence. We stop asking questions and examining. Our only criteria for determining truth becomes whether or not it fits within the spectrum of our own knowledge. This, inevitably, leads to the demonization of opposing information. It is a wise and humble man who has the willingness to question even his most cherished beliefs. This is the path of attention and vulnerability, where we daily die to hubris and dogma.

The goal, within the realm of the spirals, is not the acquisition of knowledge. Instead, the goal is a state of becoming that does not prevent us from gaining new knowledge. When we exist in this state we will naturally gain new knowledge and new perspective. We will find our way out of structures and caves and over time we will organically be approximating closer and closer to the highest form of the RIDL.

It is a process and we are a process. Incompleteness is something not to be overcome, but something to be accepted. If our quest is certainty, then we will prove the things that we think. This is a descending path that leads to self-delusion, hubris and a narrowing of perspective.

What is most important is not a set of axioms, answers or solutions. Rather, what is most important is the spectrum of our perception – the transcending of limits as to what we are able to perceive. To access big truth, we must ascend to it. We must brave the troubled water, tuning into the RIDL by exploring it from the inside rather than from a separated position from the outside.

To hold tightly to a belief, philosophy or map, is to cease to follow big truth. Only when we know not which way to go, will the path be opened up before us that leads to the RIDL.

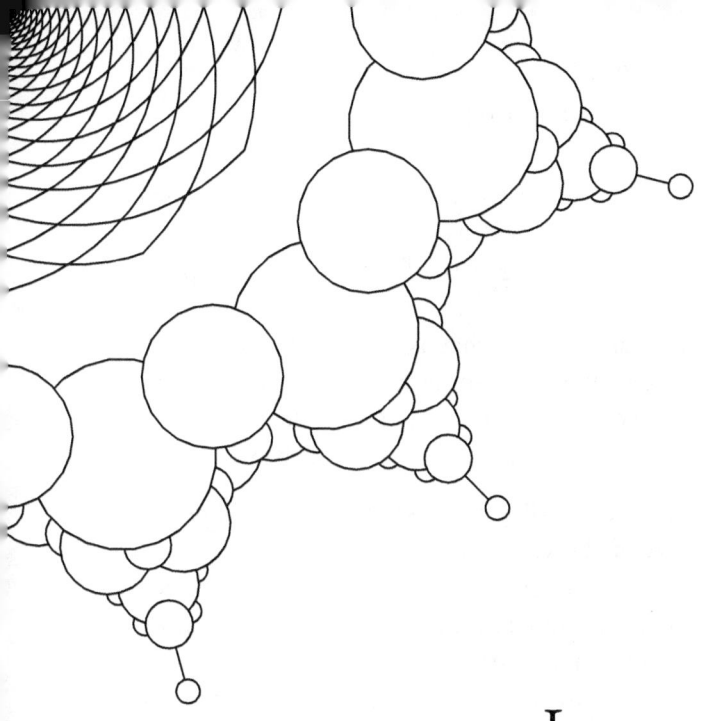

Lesson 75025

Spirals in Your Eyes

Growth is a process. As you begin to develop new eyes, what you once perceived within the confines of your narrow environments will begin to dissolve, allowing for a much deeper spectrum of understanding. Even though you will still be in the world, growth means you will become less of the world.

Time will no longer be something requiring your continual service, nor will symbols of time adorn your wrist and every wall. Rather, time will start to be seen more as opportunities – a chance to explore, experience and grow. Instead of being constantly driven by ends, you will begin to see that the most amazing part of existence is the present moment. In place of discontentment, impatience and constant manipulation of what is, you will begin to find qualities that love what is, a contentment that allows you to grow wherever you are planted and a humbleness that daily adjusts your part to the intuitive harmony of the whole.

With the expanding of perspective, you will begin to see the message of the screen that repeatedly tells you not to create for yourself. As you turn away from the screen and its sea of amusements, you will find yourself tuning in with the unlimited broadcasting station of nature. No longer will nature be seen as a cruel world struggling to survive or a futile fight against the despair of chaos and entropy; rather, it will be seen as an intricate dance with each part giving what is needed, even if what is needed is the sacrifice of a part so that new order and new forms can emerge, furthering life, even in death.

As this dance blossoms in your mind, nature will grow within as a presence to be pondered as opposed to an 'other' to be exploited. When the one starts to be seen in the many, all forms of competing interests will begin to diminish. In its place will sprout living communities – the very product of cooperation. Participating in these living communities will become more of a natural response that comes with eyes that see further.

Being more present and fully participating in what is will begin to change even the way health is viewed. Sickness will no longer simply be an enemy that must be overcome, but instead, sickness will become more like a teacher that has always been pointing to a deeper psychic pathogen that goes beyond the obvious signs and symptoms that were previously consuming our attention. Sickness will be seen more as an opportunity to learn and an opportunity to pass this knowledge on to others, even if the learning has come too late to save our part.

Your living environments will transform into something where nature no longer ends where the human begins. As the desire to eradicate nature diminishes, in its place will flourish a desire to produce it. This will be accomplished by mostly getting out of the way. As awareness grows, there will become no need to labor against soil, weeds and insects. Rather, it will become clear that, through cooperating with process, the providence of nature will give its gifts freely. Soil, weeds and insects, will then start to be seen as the life giving and healing processes that they have always been, patiently taking our abuses as they tried to get our attention. Where, formerly, you had to buy food from industrial processes, you will start to notice that food is already growing all around you. Where it was once produced in mechanical plants, now it will start to be produced more on free born plants.

As this story develops within, nature will not be the only thing that emerges. You will also start to notice the emergence of higher qualities like love and all that proceeds from it. Daily, the love for your spouse will grow, even if you have yet to meet them in this life. Love for your children will also grow, along with the love for all your relationships, whether it be your human community, or the rest of the community of life. In your home, in your relationships and in your communities, peace will come to replace quarrels. Kindness will take up residence where anger once lived. Purity will find its way into all actions, and joy will begin to infuse every moment. With the growing of perspective, a strike on the cheek will naturally cause the turning to offer the other. The taking of objects will simply mean the free giving of objects.

Laws, like Technique, encountered in every facet of your life, will begin to be viewed with greater perspective and awareness. Whereas, before, you were only capable of asking about the most appropriate and beneficial use of Technique. Now, you will find yourself asking: What problem does it solve that makes its use so indispensable? Technique may still be used, but you will find that it is using you much less as you gain awareness of its power to give direction to reality. By bringing Technique into the light, the necessary spell will start to release its grip.

As the grip of Moloch begins to loosen, your life will also begin to loosen its grip on the acquisition and multiplicity of things. In its place you will find yourself learning more about simplicity, hacking away and eliminating that which is unessential. Desire will be seen as the very thing that brought poverty to your life, distracting you and making you work harder at building the constructs of Moloch. You will come to see that poverty, in the things of Moloch, is actually the solution, allowing for the riches of higher things to well up from within. Instead of being under the spell of progress, the spirals will impel you to retreat, simplify, and to do with less rather than acquiring more.

With the decreasing consumption of Moloch's products, your need for monetary units will also decrease. By avoiding Moloch's products and the preoccupation with owning things, you will inevitably avoid the money systems required to own them. As your poverty in the eyes of Moloch grows, you will notice that your freedom will also be growing, as you will no longer be enslaved to the world of toil and self-promotion. When your time is no longer seen as money, then it will become increasingly difficult to sell it in exchange for those things that do not fill. Rather, time for you will be seen more as a gift. What you do with this gift will be your gift back to the whole.

Possessions you may still have; however, it is the attachment to possessions that will be dissolving. Consumption may still happen, but it will be consumption that is accompanied by a growing awareness of whether or not it contributes to a more beautiful whole. Where unconscious competition once reigned, conscious cooperation will now live. Sharing will start to become more valuable than the pride of accumulation, and this without the need for gratitude or repayment. Whatever you do, it will naturally become more about giving wealth to others instead of stripping it from them. In this process, you will be transforming yourself not simply into another kind of worker, but into an artist that creates a new reality that values kindness over profit. It will be the enacting of a divine economy that no longer is bound between the differing choices of Moloch's economies – the exchange of money and the fire that comes with it. This economy of spirals will be motivated by a new logic that defies the intellect of Moloch thinking, being motivated simply by a bigger view of reality.

As this larger view grows within, it will touch every aspect of your life. Government, regardless of the system that Moloch has put in place, will come to be neither feared nor praised; rather, it will come to be ignored. Your only allegiance will be to that universal law that is written on your heart, since only the law of love is worthy of your dedication. When the world and its crumbling forms collapse, you will not be under their weight. You will have transcended them, because your attention will be on the only real revolution – the growing of your part.

Through this process of growth, you will find yourself walking more with those who are growing. When you come close to truth and bump into it, you will feel compelled to give it away, sharing it freely with those who have ears to hear. In this, you will find a growing ability to distinguish those who speak words of truth. As a true teacher can do no more than become less, so that the RIDL can become more. You will also start to see with more clarity those who peddle truth for money, believing that their pocket books and their emblazoned name are far more important than the truth claimed. With time, you will come to understand that the universal wisdom of the spirals cannot be found in external sources. It will become clear that those who tell you to find it from without, in external sources, authorities or masters, are only serving themselves.

As you come out of Moloch's caves, you will find yourself becoming skeptical of both the majority and the minority, running neither towards them nor away from them. With a growing view of larger things, you will discover that it is not the place of the majority or the minority to be what influences your decisions; rather, your guide will be what is beautiful, and what aids in the developing of your consciousness.

Where, formerly, education was a preparation for making money, it will now become more of a process of self-discovery, using what has been discovered to better serve and participate in the actualization of higher qualities. Education will no longer be about making learned people, but more about implanting a desire for learning, making learning people. This will no longer require structures, institutions and paid teachers; rather, it will become a self-motivated process, void of control. Education will start taking place through participation with innumerable states, being with, as opposed to being instructed about. You will start to discover that true learning is growth, and true growth only starts to happen when you are able to come to peace with uncertainty. Humility will then show itself to be the very door that allows you to start to grapple and struggle with new ideas, new perspectives, new insights and new stories.

No longer will you feel compelled to surround yourself with only books and people that already agree with you, but instead, you will find yourself re-evaluating what you once thought you knew. Daily you will find yourself re-examining those influences that shaped your life. When reading history you will now be able to ask, whose history is it? When you learn economics you will begin to ask, whose economy is this? When you read literature, you will begin to see more clearly whose stories and constructs are being sold. Math no longer will be seen as a dry maze of abstractions to be manipulated, but rather, math will increasingly become about the mystery of numbers, and how these relate and interact with each other in amazing patterns – a symbolic reflection of the underlying geometry of life.

Even the illusion of competition that educational institutions foster will begin to fade. Raising the quality of your consciousness, growing in love and developing wisdom and understanding will become far more important than intellectual achievements directed towards a piece of embossed paper and a pay check.

Language will also begin to lose its illusory nature, being seen more as a great pointer to that rich and growing mystery that lies beyond the current picture plane. What were once merely words, will now start to be seen as cumbersome logs that you tied together in order to cross the rivers of life. Whereas, before, when you reached the other side of a river you felt compelled to carry those logs with you. Now, as your perspective grows, you will begin to feel no such compulsion. In losing your attachment to those logs, you will discover that you become much freer in your movements, finding new material along your journey when new rivers present themselves. Someday, you will arrive at the point where you realize that even tying logs together is no longer necessary.

Those logs, though, will not be despised. Rather, they will come to be seen as most necessary teachers. This is because those logs needed to be tied together and carried in order for you to realize what you were doing. You had to discover that it was you who created in your own image, and that it was you who remained unaware of this act, separating yourself from true freedom by your many attachments. Only in taking the wrong path, could the right path be revealed. This right path is the place where you drop your desire to control and know with certainty. You no longer carry logs. When this act of letting go takes place, only then do new realities begin to reveal themselves. This process will naturally begin to open up for you new worlds that are larger and more mysterious than the little worlds that your earlier mind thought it could comprehend.

Taking anything away from this dynamic, moving process called the territory – separating, measuring, and naming things, will eventually be seen as the solidifying of what cannot be made solid. In this new awareness, you will slowly begin to exist with one eye on the abstraction, with awareness of what you are using and how you are using it, and with the other eye on the mystery, that dynamic process of awe and wonder.

With these new eyes, you will begin to see more clearly even the religious distortions that come from solidifying what cannot be made solid. No longer will you exist in the many religious caves of Moloch, spending your life trying to resurrect the light that bloomed within the past. Though the morning star is beautiful, you will have come to understand that to try to capture that light is to unknowingly hew it into a thousand pieces, wasting your life and repeating the same image of those who have gone before – clinging with certainty to the fading shadows of the past.

When those scriptures are looked upon, you will not only see the profound effect that this perennial light had on the hearts of men and the movement away from the structures and spheres of Moloch, but you will also begin to see how many of those who were affected by that ancient light eventually did something unnatural to their boats. You will begin to see how they threw off their anchors and built upon the codifications of man – those testimonies and writings that inevitably appear whenever such a great light becomes manifest. It will become clear that in grasping after certainty, they focused more on the form than on its spirit, worshiping the symbols as opposed to what those symbols pointed to.

With a growing perspective, you will more easily be able to recognize that most sought after structure of certainty that now sits above those abandoned boats – a structure filled with floors and caves of doctrine and theological stances, lined with residents who believe that they have a piece of that ancient light. These residents know what God is. They know who he is as well as his name, gender and even what he requires. All this, they can prove from within their codifications. These lights and images that mesmerize the many will start to be seen for what they are: caricatures passed down from those who were victorious in the struggle between orthodoxy and heresy – the winners who wrote history and retrospectively pronounced themselves and their writings orthodox.

Whereas before, your questions revolved around whether or not this system of belief worked. Now, your questions will begin to revolve around what kind of work it has been doing, judging the correctness of its truths by the results of its application. From this new perspective, it will become increasingly seen as futile to put your hope in discovering that true light through a line of carriers that would suppress, destroy and burn documents and heretics alike – that would establish and enforce boundaries on what is and isn't scripture, on what is and isn't right doctrine – that would create creeds, doctrines, mediators, hierarchies, deacons, bishops, priests, popes and pastors – that would give birth to ecclesiastical buildings, patriarchal institutions, systems, authorities, governance, control, monetary wealth and bibliolatry – ministrations of Moloch.

So, too, will it become increasingly problematic to believe in a divine Word of God that comes to us through the medium of symbols, written words that, even when based upon the well-intended efforts of human reasoning, allow for a myriad of opposing positions that cannot be admitted by those who can only see their own position. Rather, it will become increasingly clear that if divine words and divine revelation requires critical texts, translation, interpretation and explaining, then it is us, the explainers, who ultimately become cleverer than the divine.

Believing such a thing will start to be seen as dishonoring to the RIDL, the shackling of limitless love into limited access and into an author of confusion – a mere tribal deity. Love will be seen as the very reason why language cannot be the perfect and primary vehicle of God's revelation to humanity. For if God exceeds our ability to love, then what father, who is separated from his children and desires to reunite with them, would write with words that could be distorted with the sullying influences of time, in ways that could be interpreted differently, and with words that can easily be misunderstood? What father, who exists in every moment, speaks every language, and has the ability to write to his lost children, would then write to his children in the distant past rather than the continual present, to a specific human race with a specific set of languages that cannot be perfectly communicated to his other children who do not speak those languages?

From here, your questions will only increase. If God is love, then how is it compatible with love that evil committed in time is expiated in eternity? How is it compatible with love that some are born blessed while many are born afflicted? How is it compatible with love that some come to this world with every advantage and others with none? How is it compatible with love that we have only this single life, this one chance to get it right or we will be lost in torment forever? While many will avoid these questions, declaring them as surpassing the understanding of man, it will come to be seen that to avoid these questions and submit to fear based conformity, is to ultimately make a mockery of God, of love and of justice.

Whereas before, there was certainty and rigidity in your spiritual life. Now, these will start to be replaced with humility and fluidity. No longer will you cling to the light of the past, building structures of certainty; rather, you will find yourself continually striving to get to that boat, untethering yourself from whatever framework that has been, or will be, built over you. As you pass beyond the borders of Moloch, you will then discover that the same ancient light that so many spend their lives trying to reconstruct, already exists within you, being written upon your very heart. With this new awareness, you will then no longer desire to cling to pieces of truth, nor to circumscribe those fading shadows of what was; rather, you will learn to look upon them with gratitude, recognizing them as that which resonates with the ever present light within.

With time, the path of certainty will begin to show itself as the wrong path – the path that kept your attention on outward things as opposed to inward things and on actualizing the kingdom of men as opposed to actualizing the kingdom of God. If that ancient light is anything, let it be a reminder, for we are all tasked with that same responsibility – to kindle that marvelous light within the darkness of our becoming.

We are all light bearers, buried within the depths of matter, waiting to awaken to the eternal light within. Only in becoming one with this light, harmonizing our part to that great sacred spiral, will we come to understand that it is not ours to capture the light, but to become the light.

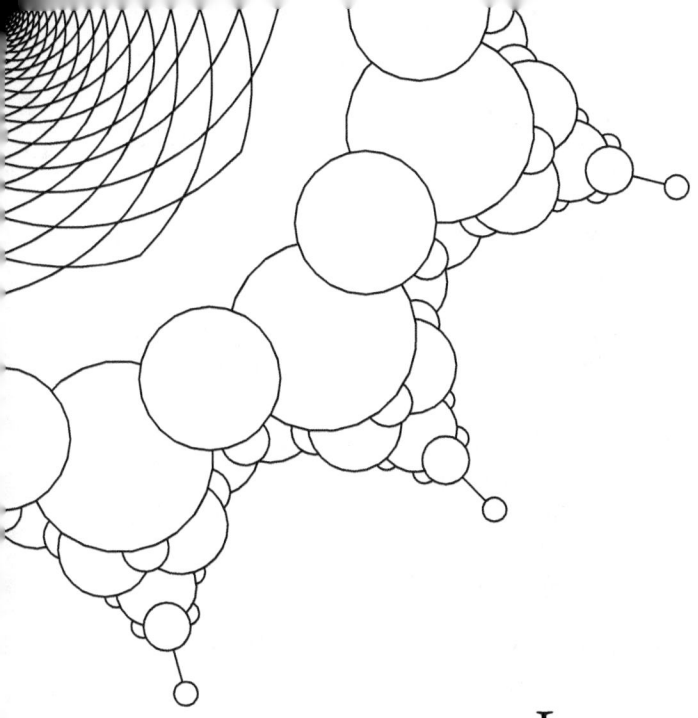

Lesson 121393

The Path of Attention

These words are the equivalent of trying to draw a golden spiral. At most, all that can be depicted, even with the most advanced tools, is an approximation that points to an archetype. This archetype cannot be reached through words, numbers or images, for who among us can count the number of phi? Models and maps hide within them a great deception that can compel you to spend your whole life working with them, lost in the illusion of control. The hope is that you will come to see through this illusion, as perfect models and maps of dynamic processes cannot exist, as they are, by definition, separate from the processes they describe. Don't spend your life trying to draw perfect spirals; rather, spend your life being drawn inward by those perfect spirals.

The beauty and grace of our necessary cycles is that these spirals have always been there to draw us in, waiting for us to notice and gain awareness of their presence, so that we could look beyond our decaying molecular forms, beyond the obstructions, distortions, concepts and attachments that so often surround us. The doors to greater perception are not difficult to find. The difficulty lies in the deconstruction of all that we have placed in the intermediary.

This story before you is not a new one. Its archetypal idea has been told throughout the ages, expressed in innumerable forms and with innumerable words and metaphors, always trying to illuminate that which prevents the emergence of these spirals. Do not become overly fixated on concepts, thinking that Moloch is only Moloch. For it is also Wetiko that possesses man for its own end. It is the Klipot that traps and encompasses pure Light. It is Ahriman that is in constant opposition to Ahura Mazda. It is the stones that fill up our bowl of Light. It is the course of Narcissus who becomes overly fixated with his own image. It is the Demiurge that shrouds Gnosis. It is Mara that allows enlightenment. It is the kingdom of man that shields itself from the kingdom of God. It is Samsara that pushes us towards Moksha. It is the outward path that distracts from the inner path. It is the hylic stage, which gives way to the psychic stage, which gives way to the pneumatic stage. It is the hiding part of hide and go seek. It is the great deceiver that prowls about like a lion. It is the clothes of truth that draws our attention away from truth. It is the technological society that obscures the metaphysical background. It is the fear of the known coming to an end. It is the pain that demands to be felt. It is the tiger above and the tiger below that keeps us from noticing the fruit in front of us. It is the weight of the soul that prevents it from ascending up through the King's Chamber. It is the wheel of life that revolves around its still point. It is the bitter cold that slowly lulls us into the sleep of death. It is the transient from which the eternal must be distilled. It is the ease of black magic. It is self-absorption that keeps us from self-reflection. It is literalism that hides the mystic path. It is ideology that distances us from curiosity. It is the house that must be pulled down to find the treasure beneath. It is the shell that must be broken to get to the kernel. It is the conceptualizing that must give way to the tasting. It is the world of spheres that maintain us within their circumference, ever obscuring the spiraled path that lies before us. It is all these things. It is many more things. And, it is none of these things.

It is none of these things because these stories are merely abstractions that are trying to point to that something beyond themselves. Abstractions are an important part of the process but they are also a dangerous part. The concept of Moloch loves to hide in abstractions. It does not fear them and actively participates in their production. It does this because it knows that those who hold to them will easily be led to further abstractions until they are, eventually, lost in a maze of doctrine and dogma, prevented from seeing what these maps were originally trying to point to. To lose sight of this pointing is to create another sphere within the realm of Moloch.

You must always attend carefully when contemplating these words, knowing that they, like the shoulders they have stood upon, are also a mere abstraction –

a crude re-emerging of that perennial story that points to what has been written upon every heart. Regardless of how many times this story has been cut down, disfigured or forgotten, it will emerge again, in different spots and in different ways, urging us to notice it, if only for a moment.

To discover the story of the spirals is not to be directed towards itself, but to that unmediated ascending movement of the inner man. There is no writing, religion, organization, master or guru that can forge a perfect map to it. There is no measurement or law that can crystallize it. This story is not a simple object that can be proven, nor is it a reservoir of certainty; rather, it is a story that must be lived – an instrument to be used and a great ally to the sleeper. If you wish to touch, taste and feel the more expanding reality that exists before you, you must not concern yourself with the externalization of this story – the proving, teaching or preaching of this message. Rather, you must be consumed with the living and embodying of it – perpetual becoming. In this way will the correctness of its truths be clearly seen. Only in the direct, unmediated contact with the spirals does the need for proof become obsolete.

Though our current layer is often tragic, understand that it is essential to experience this process. With every failure, there is meaning. In every loss, there is hope. In every tragedy, there is purpose. Your existence is the process of completing that current sentence within a much larger story that is taking shape. It is a single brush stroke that contributes to that beautiful and mysterious canvas before you. Reality is change. It is becoming. Your present stroke and your current sentence is built upon everything that has brought you to this moment. Where this story is headed, how the canvas takes shape and how the whole is becoming, greatly depends on how we write our sentences and on how aware we are of the process of painting. If we would listen, we would hear the echoes of the past urging us to write and paint well, to align our part in harmony and balance with the intuitively felt direction of a much larger whole, actualizing this higher order into reality and enriching the creative advance of the whole through the actualization of our part.

Within this process you will encounter those who write and paint poorly. Nevertheless, when you begin to see with new eyes, you will find compassion within these encounters. Compassion looks upon a perceived enemy and finds love there. It does not see an evil being, but rather, it sees a part of the whole who has yet to gain perspective and who is still lacking certain qualities within their part. Hues of the higher order will always be stronger and carry more weight than hues of the lower order. Well written letters, words and sentences, though they may be few, carry with them a force that reverberates throughout the entire work. When we love instead of hate, pursue peace instead of war, forgive instead of taking insult, give in place of receiving, are faithful in the face of temptation, turn from evil instead of embracing it and dance with our children instead of ignoring them, we unleash a vital force to which darkness can only smile. Darkness, the great hidden carrier of light.

This is the same force that waits to be actualized within each and every manifestation, within each and every node that span out upon this fractaling net of infinite potentiality. It is upon this net, with every exhale and inhale of the RIDL, that reality comes in and out of existence, undulating its shimmering fractals, learning, growing, becoming and constantly re-configuring itself based upon the actualization of its parts – a never ending movement of descending into individualization and ascending into realization.

Within our current reality, we possess an immense responsibility to create, to actualize, to write and to paint with awareness of our co-creative link with the dynamically evolving, multidimensional whole – a whole that is simultaneously creating and being created by. Creation is not a point in the past, but a point in the moving present. It is a movement of that which is above and that which is below, both possessing that innate impulse to create and grow by experiencing and discovering itself. That which is above is consciousness and that which is below is consciousness, each reflecting each other and acting upon the necessity to resonate, modify, evolve and change – reflecting intelligence back to intelligence and consciousness back to consciousness.

Strive to actualize those higher qualities within your part, revealing and not concealing what every fiber of your being compels you to bring forth. The very nature of light is to illuminate that which is not light. Only in being unconscious of this process is evil able to grow. Within darkness is the revelation of light. By making ourselves conscious of the darkness, we are thus illuminated by it. It is only through the darkness that the RIDL is able to see itself.

Within this great abyss of unconsciousness, where the collective psychosis of Moloch feeds and reinforces itself through each unwitting part, know that to step away from this destructive path is to be perceived as being outside of the collective. Though you may, at times, feel quite lonely, strive to see with greater clarity the creations of Moloch – the images and thoughts that have flickered throughout our minds, trapping us within the many environments of our own creation.

If you are reading this and find yourself to be infected, simply begin to achieve some semblance of stillness within your life. Stop feeding the psychic pathogen and its thought forms. Instead, learn from them. Moloch is a marvelous teacher that will, if allowed, compel you to the place of inward stillness where you will find waiting for you the perennial story that longs to heal and reunite with that which was necessary to separate from. Hearts will forever remain restless until they find the true rest that only comes through reunion.

There is, within you, a sanctuary. Protect this place. For nothing can usurp authority over this place that rightly belongs to your part. Reorder this inner sanctuary so that you are not ruled by distractions, by those things that do not truly satisfy. Discover and experience the inner light that is written throughout your being and then actualize it into reality as faithfully as possible. Allow yourself to be animated by this light and let love, and what proceeds from it, have the highest order in your life. Quiet yourself, meditate, pray and rediscover nature and its beautiful patterns.

Know that it is not ours to control but only to create. What we create is entirely based upon what type of story resides within. The one constant of creation is that it is movement. Movement is either drawn towards harmony or away from it. Stories are powerful. You will create them and they will create you. So do not be apathetic, for regardless of the movement you choose, by it you will be created.

The hope of these many words is that they will be an aid to help you in discovering the freedom that comes with moving towards harmony. Freedom starts by examining all things, understanding why you do the things you do, why you believe what you believe. The ideas you hold to will always affect you. There are consequences to thought. Belief is unavoidable and the story you believe in will have an immeasurable effect on your life. So be wise.

Freedom inevitably longs to free others. When you begin to glimpse that marvelous light, be patient and wise with those you desire to share it with. Though many will, for a time, be content with distractions and lower things, being bound by the sense world and its surface-intellect, understand that it is the height of irresponsibility to drag someone into the darkness who is not ready. Doing so will only produce more comfortable seats, making their need for control stronger. Rather, rest in the hope that fate will eventually guide both the willing and the unwilling. Focus on your part, letting that marvelous light shine through you uninhibited. Ultimately, it may be your inner light that causes a resident to glance back, if only for a moment.

Take note of what often happens when you begin following those beautiful spirals to where they lead. When one pillar of established truth falls, others quickly come down with it, as if one is affecting the other. Yet, to those around you, it will seem as if you are of the most destructive sort, actively seeking other pillars to destroy for the sheer pleasure in it, having no insight into the sincerity of your quest and the difficulty that comes with overturning established ideas.

Know that the further humanity drifts away from the RIDL, the more they will hate those who embody it. Those who are free from Moloch's grip become a danger to everything that is unessential. There will always be communal consequences for dissension, yet understand that to dissent, when confronted with discord, is of much value. Many have gladly suffered to be faithful to the soul's quest for understanding. It is the love of becoming that bids us to journey on what can often be a very difficult and lonely road.

Finally, to each one of you, know that we have loved you with a love that transcends time and defies this feeble attempt at human language and emotion. Even if we are no longer physically present within your current layer, know that we are still very much present. When you begin to see with new eyes, you will start to see just how close we truly are.

– A Spiral Becoming

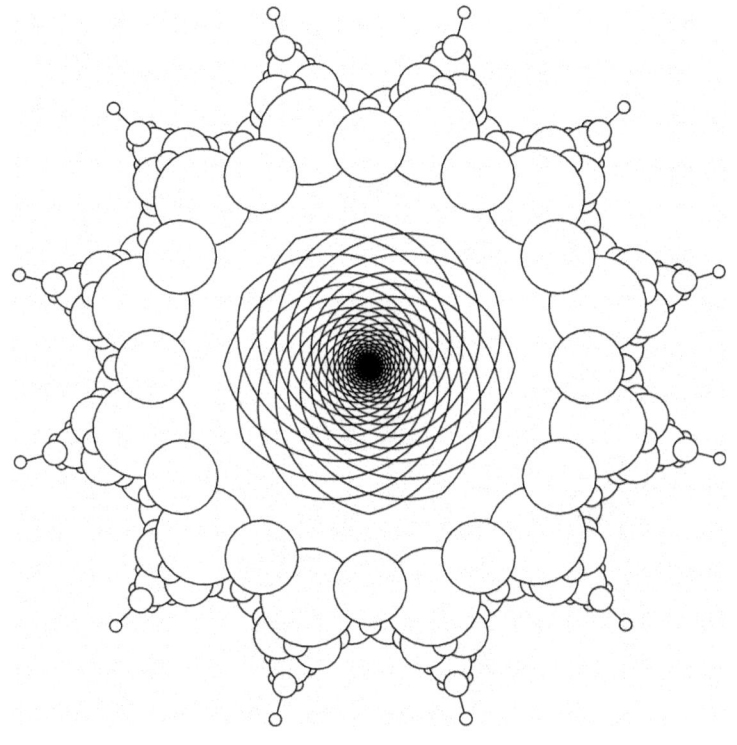

www.ingramcontent.com/pod-product-compliance
Lightning Source LLC
Chambersburg PA
CBHW051931160426
43198CB00012B/2102